# SKI TOURING IN CALIFORNIA

## BY DAVID BECK

First Edition 1972
Second Edition 1980
Copyright © 1972, 1980 by David Beck
Formerly published as *Ski Tours in California*
Cover photo by David Beck
Back cover photo by Susan Beck
Inside photos by David Beck except as noted
Design by Marshall Crossman
Library of Congress Card Catalog Number 83-51473
International Standard Book Number 0-89997-034-6
Printed in the United States
Published by Wilderness Press
         2440 Bancroft Way
         Berkeley, CA 94704

           Write for free catalog

## Acknowledgements

The following people helped make this book possible: Gar Baring of the U.S.S.A., Jake Beck, Greg Beserra of Robbins Mountain Shop, Michael Chessler of Sierra West, Wes Chormicle of Sports & Trails, Ned Dairiki, John Fischer of Palisade School of Mountaineering, Bill Faulhaber, Bruce Hart of Mountain Sports, Nick Hartzell, Gary Kirk of Caribou, Phil Kerridge of China Peak, Barbara Lilley, Jim Owens of Smilie Co., Steve O'Mera of Arcata Transit, Loyd Price of Yosemite Mountaineering, Steve Wilkie, Galen Rowell, Doug Robinson, Bob Swanson of Sierra Designs, Bill Simm, Knut Waarli, Lief Voeltz of Fifth Season, Norm Wilson, Steve Weldon of Sonora Mountaineering, and John Juan Bagley for his photographic help, Debby Shishkoff for the map art and Claudia Beck for the illustrations.

The following people helped review the manuscript and offered valuable advice: Rick Robinson on Wax, Carl Martin for the sections on Snow and Avalanches, David Wasniewski on Technique. Doug Patrick and Mary Pipersky for general comments and to Willi Fuller and Lynne Short who found the errors.

Special thanks to Ella Tieslau who shared her home and to Lolita who kept us in tostadas. And special thanks to Sam King for his encouragement. Finally, to Marshall Crossman for her amazo dedication to this project.

# Ski Touring In California

The winter is special. Each new snowfall provides a fresh un-tracked world to explore. Ski touring is the best way to travel over the snow. Skiing is ancient. No one knows when the first ice age hunter strapped on a pair of skis; petroglyphs indicate it was at least 4,000 years ago. There is a sense of antiquity, a feel of history about ski touring. Skiing is exhilarating. Before steam engines or aircraft, the fastest people in the world were skiers.

Why go ski touring? Maybe you don't like to stand in lift lines. It takes an expert powder skier to know that nordic skiers ski more powder than alpine skiers. You may like to race; nordic racers are among the most physically fit people in the world. If you have children, you may want to ski with them and share their wonder at seeing snow for the first time.

California is the very best place to be if you are a cross country skier. In the early 1970's when the first edition of this book was written, nordic skiing was just catching on. There weren't many ski shops or touring centers for the nordic skier. Today touring is the fastest growing winter sport in California. Now there are ski shops throughout the state where you can rent or buy the latest in nordic equipment. There are now ski touring centers where you can rent equipment, take lessons and ski maintained trail systems.

It's easy to get started. Marked trails are beginning to appear in the National Parks and Forests. You can ski along the rim of Yosemite Valley or through the Giant Sequoias. Skiing through the Bristlecone Pines in the White Mountains gives you a feeling for the high desert. Southern California is unique; where else can skiers drive through orange groves on their way to the snow? The Sierra Nevada has superb ski mountaineering opportunities. Spring skiing is excellent; Californians can ski into June. Almost every roadhead in the mountains ends in a quiet snowbound meadow.

This guide book is designed to help you whether you're a beginner or a seasoned skier. In addition to the suggested tours there are complete sections on equipment, ski technique, reading the snow and route finding. Different touring areas are described in general terms. Other tours are described in detail because of their special features and they are good places to start. This guide will introduce you to an area, and show you how to travel intelligently and safely. Routes vary according to the time of year, the amount of snowfall, and even the time of day. The only limits on where to ski are those imposed by your own imagination and ability.

I hope this book will help you appreciate and enjoy the California winter. It's been fun writing it. This ski touring guide is the culmination of many peoples' skiing experiences. I would appreciate any comments or ideas.

*David Beck*

David Beck
Sierra Ski Touring
P.O. Box C – 9
Mammoth Lakes, California 93546

# Table of Contents

Photo: Armando Menocal

# Starting Out

First impressions are important. Don't start a beginner on an overnight tour with borrowed gear which doesn't fit. Easy day tours are best. Before you take off, read the sections on clothing and technique as well as the check lists concerning equipment, repair, and first aid. Take this book with you; it's meant to be used as you ski along.

Many novice skiers choose a destination which is too difficult and they return to their starting point after dark feeling cold and tired. If your group has energetic members who are pushing it, stop by a hillside and let them practice downhill technique while others have a long lunch. The slowest member of your party should set the pace. Remember, it takes about three days to acclimate and to become familiar with your skis. Keep your group together. It's easy to become lost in unfamiliar territory. Allow plenty of time for your return trip. Ironically, beginners take longer to go downhill than uphill.

Leave word of your destination and route with a reliable source. Help will come more quickly if rescuers know where to look. Many rescue parties won't start out at night; they wait for morning. So a tour party should be able to spend a night out. There is a saying among ski instructors that if you carry emergency gear you never need it. In some areas there are many day skiers and even nordic ski patrols so you don't have to be as prepared for emergencies as you would in more remote areas.

Here are basic trail manners which are important anywhere:
* Report all accidents and give what help you can.
* Obey all trail signs and posted warnings.
* Faster skiers have the right-of-way. If a skier shouts "track on your right" step to the left and let him or her pass.
* Ski safely and in control. There is never any reason to collide with another skier.
* Do not stop or obstruct a trail in steep areas or where you are not visible to others.

* Fill all the sitzmarks you make. Help maintain the track.
* If you go skiing with a dog, stay out of tracks that other skiers use.
* Trails may be closed because of races, avalanche hazard or other reasons, stay off them. Respect private property.
* Pick up litter. Keeping ski touring areas clean is everyone's responsibility.
* Latrine areas should be at least fifty meters from any stream, lake, camp or trail. Please burn or carry out toilet paper.
* Crossed skis placed upright in the snow are the universal distress signal.

## Skis

Skis come in different sizes and shapes. There are racing, light touring, medium touring, mountain and alpine skis. Nordic skis should reach up to your wrist or palm when you stand with your arm stretched above your head. Alpine skiers prefer shorter skis. Longer skis glide and float over soft snow better than shorter skis which are easier to turn.

Racing skis are light. Lightweight gear is essential to a racer who has to run on skis for many kilometers. Narrow racing skis have less friction than wider skis and they are less apt to catch in a ski track. Training skis are slightly heavier than racing skis. Like racing skis they are designed for use in groomed tracks.

Most nordic skiers use light touring skis. They are suitable for racing or off-track skiing. Medium touring and mountain skis are not used so much now. They are stable in soft snow and will float better than a light touring ski, but they are heavier. We skied the John Muir Trail on metal-edged light touring skis which worked very well.

Camber gives a ski the bow shape. When you weight a ski, the camber is flattened and weight is distributed along the ski's length. Racing skis have lots of camber so they will glide on the tips and tails. The middle of the ski, where the running wax is, only touches the snow when it is pushed down during the kick. Off-track skis have less camber so they will be easier to turn. Heavier skiers need more camber in their skis. As a general rule, you should be able to squeeze a pair of touring skis together with one hand.

Ski flexibility is important to tips and tails so the ski will turn and slide over bumps and gullies. Alpine touring skis usually have no camber and have soft tips. Torsional rigidity is important. Hold a ski in the middle and twist the tip with your other hand. You can feel the torsional rigidity. This is critical to a ski's design, it enables the ski to glide and turn properly. A ski with not enough rigidity will ski like a noodle and be worthless on ice or hard snow.

Sidecut is important for skis intended to be used off the track. The ski is wider at the tip and tail than in the middle. It is this hourglass design which helps the ski to turn. Rock a ski to one side to set an edge and the ski will turn along the arc of the sidecut. Alpine skis have a lot of sidecut while racing skis have little or none.

Alpine touring skis are easier to turn. They are also heavy. Good skiers can use light touring skis with metal edges for most of the alpine tours in this book; they lose some time descending but they climb much faster with nordic gear. Ski design is always in a state of change. New kinds of skis combining the lightweight and flat skiing capabilities of nordic with the stability and maneuverability of alpine skis are starting to appear. It's an interesting time of change in the art of making cross-country skis.

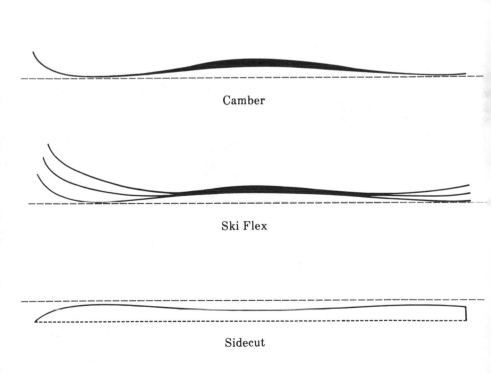

Camber

Ski Flex

Sidecut

## Boots

One of the keys to nordic skiing is good boots. They must protect your feet. Warmth and comfort are important. Be sure your boots are long enough; your toes should not touch the front of the boot. Boots which are too big will be sloppy and make ski control difficult. Boots have torsional rigidity, and a soft boot will make it difficult to ski the flats and impossible to ski downhill. Beginners can save themselves frustration if they select stiff-soled boots. Try to get a boot sole that isn't too slippery. Racers must have light and flexible shoes. As of 1979, touring boots for the 38 or 50 mm bindings suitable for off-track skiing are not available.

## Bindings

The 75 mm nordic pin bindings are almost universally used. There are three pins in the binding that fit into three holes in the toe of your ski boot. A bail holds the boot welt down on the binding. There are disadvantages to the 75 mm binding. They extend over the sides of the skis and sometimes catch on icy tracks or during turns. The good points about the 3-pin binding are that their design is simple and durable. It is difficult to find bindings that allow you to use hiking boots. Cable bindings are awkward. A lightweight, universal binding which would fit regular boots or walking shoes would be useful.

Ski mountaineering bindings have two modes: one with a free heel for climbing and one where the heel locks for skiing downhill. Ski mountaineers have a variety of bindings to choose from. The Ramer and Silveretta 400 are good. A skier will always have more control and security using alpine touring gear, rather than nordic, but there is a weight penalty. Alpine touring gear weighs almost three times as much as nordic. Most mountain tourers use 3-pin bindings. Alpine gear is used for ski tours like Mount Shasta or Lamarck Col. The lighter 50 mm or 38 mm bindings work well for track skiing.

Heel locators have become very popular among nordic skiers. Locators consist of a small spur attached to the heel of the boot. The spur fits into a slot attached to the ski. Locators give good downhill control because a boot cannot slide off a ski. However, very soft shoes will come down on a ski outside the slot and then it's impossible to put the heel on the ski without lifting it and placing it in the slot. The locators are no substitute for good boots. There have been several accidents in the California backcountry because of locators. Heels have been locked to skis under certain snow or downhill conditions. If skis don't release in a fall, you can twist your ankle or leg.

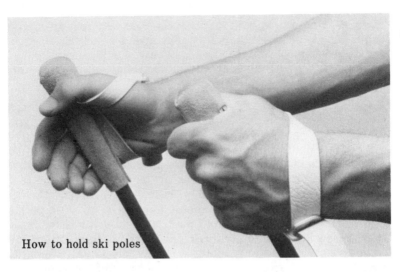

How to hold ski poles

## Poles

Ski poles are normally made of bamboo. Be sure they are strong: bamboo poles come in different widths. Nylon strapping tape wrapped around a bamboo pole every five inches, will make it much stronger. Ski racers use very lightweight poles made of carbon fiber. Mountain skiers use strong aluminum alloy poles. Serious ski mountaineers use ski poles which will screw together and work as avalanche probe poles. Wide powder baskets are handy; use lightweight plastic ones.

## Clothing

Plan on falling; it's part of skiing. Wear clothes that will stay dry when you fall. Wool or synthetics such as nylon make the best garments. Choose material that will keep you warm when damp. Long underwear, such as Lifa, is made of polypropylene and works very well. It is extremely lightweight and will keep you warm and dry. Don't overdress. Heavy parkas and sweaters will spend most of their time in your pack. Light, warm clothing is best. Nordic skiing is a complete exercise; skiing warms you up. Ski tourers are constantly adding or subtracting layers; a great excuse for a rest stop.

Either knickers or long pants are fine for nordic skiing. Gaiters, either long or short, are essential; long are better for extended ski trips, they keep your knicker socks or pant legs dry and your legs warm. Make sure they fit; you don't want snow down your shoes. Gaiters that are waterproof from the boot down are fine, but don't get full-length waterproof ones. Moisture will condense on the inside and make your socks damp.

Ears and fingers get cold fast and the best way to stay comfortable is to keep them warm. Gloves aren't nearly as warm as mitts; heavy wool or nylon fleece is best. Keep an extra pair in your pack. Wear light overmitts; your mitts will stay dry and warm.

Your body will divert warmth to your brain and vital organs at the expense of arms and legs. It's a cliche, but it's true, "If your feet are cold, put on your hat." A thick wool cap should cover your ears. Wind takes heat away from you. For instance, if the temperature is 30°F and there is a twenty mile-an-hour wind, the windchill equivalent temperature is 0°F. Protection from moisture, wind, snow, and rain is critical. A warm parka with a hood is necessary on cold days or overnight trips. A pair of nylon wind pants and a wind shell are good investments. A cagoule is a lightweight, waterproof, loose-fitting garment that pulls over the head and comes down to the knees. When it's cold and wet, cagoules are wonderful. Waterproof overgarments sweat when you work in them and non-waterproof garments leak. You get damp regardless. A tightly-woven cotton such as Ventile works well. Gor-Tex, a new fabric, allows vapor to pass through it, but will shed water. Gor-Tex garments must be washed frequently and the seams must be sealed.

The ski clothing industry is beginning to supply a variety of functional and fashionable garments for the nordic skier. Bib knickers, one-piece suits, knicker-jacket combinations are designed with different skiers in mind. Racers need the light-

Photo:
Gordon Wing

weight stretch suits, while day tourers can choose from thin-sulate, pile and other synthetic blends made to give maximum  freedom of movement plus various degrees of warmth. Synthetics shed snow, an important consideration even for skiers out for the day. Cotton is ok for a day tour in the spring when there's lots of sun and no danger if you do get wet. Wool, the traditional favorite, is great especially in the cold winter months.

## Kids

Nordic skiing is a family sport. Babies in packs, small children on smaller skis, even teenagers like being out on the trails. When you take a child skiing, a lesson is a good idea. Try to find a nordic ski school that will put him or her in a class with other children. While kids have their lesson, parents should disappear. If you prefer to teach them yourself, be patient and encouraging and you'll both have a good time. Very young children, four years and up, can learn basic skiing.

Children do best on the same kind of equipment you have, nordic shoes and pin bindings. Adjustable cables where a child uses his or her own boots work, but they are awkward and are difficult to adjust. There are skis for young children with leather bindings that come as part of the ski. These are good for very young children, but they are usually wood skis that you must wax. In California with changeable snow conditions waxless skis work best for kids. Children are not interested in technique and wax requires technique. Whether to rent or buy equipment depends on how often you go skiing. If you live in the mountains or go skiing frequently, buy the necessary gear. You can always trade or sell the skis and boots at a local ski swap. You can get children's shoes for pin bindings as small as a size ten. Flexible fiberglass waxless skis are best. Get a longer ski than necessary and use them for several years. Sometimes a longer ski helps ... there is more ski to float on and kids fall less. Poles should come to a child's armpit and bamboo poles are fine. If your children are seven or eight, they can carry a small day pack and be responsible for their own treats, water and extra clothing.

Show them how to use their poles for balance. We don't encourage children to use pole-straps. They are hard to get on and off over mittens and when they fall it is a struggle to get the poles off so they can get up. When they fall, and they will right away, let them get up by themselves. This is hard, it's much easier to give a hand. But they will come to expect it and you will spend half your time picking them up and they may never learn how to get up. Explain before you put the skis on that everyone falls when they ski, beginners and experts alike and that everyone gets up by themselves. Have them put on their own skis as soon as they are old enough. Show them how the binding works; the sooner they learn the happier you'll be. Let them carry their own skis and poles. The more self-sufficient you encourage them to be the faster they'll improve and enjoy ski touring. With patience and encouragement children can do great things on skis.

Children aren't interested in technique; they just want to get moving. Balance is important. Have them walk in your tracks keeping their skis parallel; then let them be leader and you follow. Show them how to turn on the flat. Demonstrate step turns and walking so that their skis never cross. Look for a very gentle hill. It's difficult for children to get their skis pointed downhill on a sidehill; their skis start down before they're ready and they fall. If you can, find a hill with a flat top so they can get in position to ski down.

Going downhill is fun; the best part of skiing no matter what age you are. Let them go straight downhill over and over; don't worry about learning how to stop or turn. Let them get the feel and thrill of skiing. Sometimes if kids have trouble going downhill without falling, we have them leave their poles behind and go down with their hands on their knees. This gets them in a proper position. We also have them place their feet about six to eight inches apart for better stability. When they feel comfortable, show them how to stop and turn. Use the same technique you would. If they try hard and can't do it, try something else. Go on a short tour, let them lead, stop for a snack. They'll pick it up when they're ready. Side-stepping is one of the hardest things to teach a child. When you have to go up a narrow or short but steep place, tell them to be patient, and make sure their skis are sideways on the hill before taking short steps up or down the hill. All technique should be mixed with a tour. Pick a nearby destination; you will be amazed how slow a five year old can be. Even seven or eight year olds think a mile is a very long way. On the tour the child sets the pace.

Clothing is important. Many parents dress kids in cotton: underpants, longjohns and levis. Cotton doesn't work; kids fall and get wet and cold. If you dress them in cotton be sure to put nylon overpants and a jacket on. Dress them in wool hats, wool mittens and sweaters. Don't over-dress them either. It is important that children stay dry. Sunglasses are hard to find for children but they're important. Their eyes are sensitive and must be protected; they don't know enough to realize their eyes are in danger from the light. The same care is needed for their skin, use lots of sunscreen.

If a child's energy or interest flags, try games. When learning to ski, mix in games designed for children such as Red Rover, Fox and Geese, Tag. If they would like to race, set up relay teams on the flat and slalom gates on the hill. Use their poles for gates. When they get older you may want to show them the map and point out your location and destination. If they're interested, show them a compass. Children love beginning orienteering providing you make a game of it. By eight on up children should be taught about hypothermia. What to do if lost (stay put) and how to build a shelter. It's fun to build a snowcave or igloo. Sleep in it overnight. Make them feel at home in the winter. Appreciation of the environment comes with understanding and the feeling of accomplishment. If they don't enjoy touring, don't feel you failed. We know some nine year olds who hated the sport when they were six and who are now excellent skiers. Have a good time.

Photo: Tom Burns

# Winter Safety

On a tour in the Sierra you should be prepared for rain, temperatures below zero and snowfall of five feet in one storm. The success of any ski tour depends on how well prepared you are for changes in the weather and possible emergencies. There is no substitute for a first aid course and the ones offered by the American Red Cross are excellent. For more information on mountaineering first aid and rescue, please refer to the bibliography.

**Sunburn.** Everyone is glad to see the sun come out after a storm. You get out of the tent and dry your gear and clothing. However, be careful of the sun. Especially on spring tours, you can get badly sunburned. Reflected light will burn ears, nose and even the inside of your mouth. John Muir was right when he called the Sierra "The Range of Light." The sun dominates our climate. Skin cancer research is done by studying professional skiers. Use lots of sunscreen; those that have PABA (parabenzoic acid) work best. Rub it over your face, ears, lips and hands repeatedly during the day. In the spring at high elevations you need a hat that will shield all of your head. Use a baseball cap with a bandana to protect ears and neck as well as eyes. A bandana over your face, outlaw style, is sometimes the only way to protect your nose.

**Snow Blindness.** If the snow seems bright and you squint even with sunglasses on, you are getting snowblind. At night your eyes feel like they have sand in them. Carry an extra pair of good glasses. They don't have to be expensive but they must be dark. Some plastic lenses distort vision, causing eyestrain. If your glasses are not dark enough, put tape on the lenses leaving thin horizontal and vertical slits to see through. Tape the sides of your glasses to keep out light from the side. Duct or electricians tape works fine. If your glasses get broken, fashion a pair of eskimo glasses by cutting slits in a piece of stiff cardboard.

**Frostbite and Frostnip.** Frostbite occurs when a part of the body, usually toes or fingers, is frozen. Severe frostbite is rare. Frostnip, however, is fairly common. Frostnip is a prelude to frostbite; the skin is not yet frozen and it turns gray and has a waxy appearance. When the weather is cold and windy, members of a touring party should watch one another for frostnip. If a skier's nose, ears or cheeks show the signs of frostnip, he or she should be promptly warmed. *Never* rub frostnipped or frostbitten skin and *absolutely never* soak affected parts in gasoline. Warm chilled fingers by putting them in your armpits. If your feet become frostbitten when you are far from

help it is better to ski on them while still frozen rather than
thaw them out. Once they are thawed you cannot ski or walk.
Frostbite should always be treated as a bad burn and always
see a doctor because of the risk of infection and gangrene. To
avoid frostbite, be sure your shoes and mitts are not too tight.
You should be able to wiggle your toes and fingers and feel
them. If you can't, stop and warm up.

**Hypothermia.** This condition is a drop in body temperature. It
occurs when the body loses heat faster than it can produce it.
At first someone suffering from hypothermia shivers and
stumbles about. As his body temperature falls, he becomes
irrational and eventually falls into a stupor. With a core
temperature below 78° the heart and respiratory system stop
working.

To prevent hypothermia stay dry and out of the wind. During
the winter it can rain anytime and anywhere in California, so
carry waterproof outer clothing that will keep you dry. Carry a
rainfly for your tent. Wear wool or other material that will re-
tain warmth even when wet. Carry quick energy food to keep
up your strength. During strenuous exercise the body pro-
duces up to ten times the energy it does at rest. Both exercise
and food will increase body heat.

If your party finds itself in a situation where someone seems
possibly hypothermic, don't panic. Find a sheltered spot and
put up your tent or improvise a shelter out of your equipment.
Remove his wet clothing and put on dry, then put him in a
sleeping bag. Build a fire. If the person is very cold, remove his
or her clothing and the clothing of another warm person. Have
them climb in a sleeping bag together. They should stay
together until the cold person is thoroughly warmed, possibly a
few hours. Warm drinks help psychologically, but won't increase body warmth.

**Injuries.** If a nordic skier is injured, chances are there is no ski
patrol to take care of him. Always plan in advance what to do if
someone in your party is hurt or becomes ill. If a member cannot continue, do everything you can to keep him warm.
Carefully lift the victim into a sleeping bag. Be sure he is insulated from the snow; put packs and extra clothing, even skis,
under him. Broken bones should be well splinted. Immobilize
the joints on each side of the broken bone. An inflatable plastic
splint will work best. A full-leg plastic splint can also be used
for a broken arm. Never transport an injured person unless
you have sufficient manpower, equipment and experience to do
it safely. First aid requires knowing what not to do, as well as
what to do. A seriously injured or sick skier in shock, must

*never* be left alone. If you have checked out with someone responsible, help will eventually come. If someone goes for help alone, he or she must ski very cautiously. In an emergency it is easy to push too hard and get lost or have another accident. A safe party should have at least four members.

When you think of safety think in terms of the rule of three. Generally, a person can live three minutes without air, three hours without warmth, three days without water and three weeks without food.

## Snowcamping

Day tours are a bit of a tease. Just when things begin to get interesting it's time to turn back. You always wonder what's around the next bend or over the next ridge. In Europe there are extensive hut systems for wandering skiers. Unfortunately, in California there are few huts. On a cold December night it is certainly warmer and cozier to settle in a small cabin with a pot-belly stove than a tent.

Snow camping is a skill. Cold fingers and feet, thirst and sunburn, uncertainties of route finding and skiing with a pack are just some of the unpleasantries to master. California has vast snowy regions, much of it wilderness. Snow camping is the only way to visit these areas. In winter you could travel from Carson Pass to Walker Pass and never remove your skis to cross a road, a distance of over 250 miles. Snow campers must travel light and yet must not forget essential items. Some ski tourers carry seventy pound packs for weekend tours while others have been rumored to head out on four-day tours with twenty-five pound packs. These are extremes; there's a middle road. The gear listed in the equipment list is actually used on trans-Sierra tours.

**Gear.** Softpacks have replaced frames among most backcountry skiers. With a good waistbelt a softpack rides comfortably and isn't top heavy, wobbly or likely to catch on limbs. Packs are like boots; different makes fit differently. Your pack must be comfortable. A pack's center of gravity should be close to your back; load heavy items to the front. It's better to have a large pack three-quarters full than a small pack over-stuffed and uncomfortable.

Foam pads are important. Cold snow will conduct heat away from your body much faster than air will. You need at least a half-inch thick foam pad. A combination of a covered closed and open cell foam pad is worth its weight. Some skiers carry a large pad plus small pads to fit under hips and shoulders.

A warm dry sleeping bag is more than a luxury; it's a necessity. You need at least two-and-one-half pounds of down or over three pounds of dacron. Under the driest conditions snow camping is damp. In fact, you should always be drying your gear. Wet mitts and socks dry out in your bag at night. During a warm afternoon always take a long lunch and dry your sleeping bag. Down is worthless when wet and it is difficult to keep dry in winter. Bags made of PolarGuard or Hollofil II dry almost instantly, they don't really get wet. However, bags with synthetic fill are heavy and bulky. Synthetic fillers tend to break down. Loft is the thickness of a bag; the more loft, the warmer the bag.

There are expensive down bags available with Gor-Tex shells. Skiers who have used them are very pleased. With care, the down stays dry. A few skiers use the double vapor barrier (DVB) system with down bags. They use a waterproof cover and liner and the bag cannot get wet. During warm weather a DVB is like a sauna. However, in cold weather the DVB works very well. It also lessens dehydration, a serious winter problem. The DVB system can also keep feet warm. Wear a lightweight wool sock, a strong plastic bag, a heavy wool sock, another plastic bag, and finally your boot. The wool sock between the two bags will stay dry regardless of how wet your boot or foot gets.

Snowcamping below Elizabeth Pass
Sierra High Route

**Campsites.** The art of snow camping shows most when camp is pitched. Everything goes smoothly. Tents go up, a stove is lit and tea is ready in minutes. The experienced snow camper is never in a hurry yet things seem to get done.

Camp early; it's never fun cooking in the dark. A good campsite is on a forested knoll near running water and firewood. It is protected from frosty valley winds. Never camp under a tree that could snow-bomb a tent. Never camp in an avalanche path. An ideal snow camp also has a view and gets early morning sun. If possible, camp where you can ski out safely if a big storm hits. If you can't, you will have to sit out a storm or avalanche period.

Skipack tent sites. On new snow you may have to footpack and then skipack the site. If you don't, during the night you will come to know every bump; tent sites must be hard and level. Use skis and poles for tent pegs. Small twigs buried and foot-packed will also hold guy lines. Everything goes into plastic bags and keep the bags where you can find them when it snows.

Snowcamping in Upper Deadman Canyon
Sierra High Route

There is nothing like a campfire in winter. However, never have a fire near a summer use area or near timber line where wood is scarce. Fire will burn its way into the snow. Use a shovel and dig a platform down around it. Obey all camping regulations. When you go on an overnight tour, get a permit. Permit systems are the only way government authorities can measure winter use. Ski tourers are independent which is the way it should be. However, land will be "used"; if not for ski tourers then for snowmobiles and resorts.

**Shelter.** You need a tent. Snow caves or igloos are not always possible. The snow may be too hard, too soft or too shallow. You can get by with a bivouac sack, but in a storm tents are far better. Large three or four person tents are roomy and comfortable.

The basic requirements for a tent are:
* It must stand up to the winds and hold the snow loads which you will someday meet.
* You must be able to pitch it quickly without taking your mitts off.
* If a pole is broken or lost, you must still be able to pitch the tent.
* It must be well made. Are the seams neat? Stitching tight and secure? Is a double-needle sewing machine used on important seams? Are there loose panels that will flap in the wind?
* Does the tent frost up in cold weather?
* How much does it weigh?
* Is it rainproof?

Caves or igloos are the best of all shelters. They are warm and comfortable. However, they take a few hours to construct. Caves are quicker to build than igloos. Dig an entrance trench in a hillside until it is chest deep. Then dig sleeping spaces at right angles. Now roof the "T" shaped trench. Skis and poles make good roof supports. After the snow sets up, the skis may be removed. A lightweight, inexpensive space blanket makes a good no-drip roof. To conserve warmth, walls and ceiling should be at least six inches thick. A candle will keep a snowcave or igloo warm regardless of the temperature.

Igloos are built in a spiral. One person in the middle builds the igloo; those on the outside cut the blocks. Find an area where there has been some wind and it's possible to cut good blocks. After the final snow block is placed on top, an entrance way is cut into the igloo. Pack snow into all cracks and smooth the outside of your igloo or cave. There should be a vent at the top and in the door, at least as wide as a ski basket; carbon monoxide is formed by gas stoves and when it doesn't kill, it certainly can leave a bad headache.

**Cooking.** Gas or kerosene work best in cold weather. Butane doesn't perform well in cold weather, propane is heavy and alcohol stoves are not warm enough. Avoid using stoves in tents or snow caves. One mistake lighting a stove and a flare will singe eyebrows and melt tent walls. More tents are destroyed by stove fires than by any other cause. You must be very careful when cooking in a tent. Stoves and pots must be stable. One person should hold a cooking pot while another cooks. Scalds from spilled pots are painful and can cause serious injuries. A light piece of plywood will make a good stove platform, and, as a matter of fact, so will this book.

Lighting a stove should be a careful ritual. Do it outside or where a flare will have a minimal effect. Be sure the tank is full. Cleaning needles should be handy in case the orifice plugs. Be sure all fuel bottles are tightly capped. Place the stove on its platform, pump it and release a small amount of fuel to prime it. Some stoves have to be primed with an eyedropper. Too much priming and it will flare. Light the fuel and let it burn until it's almost out. Turn the stove on a little bit; the small flame will warm the stove and build pressure. Pump the stove again and turn it up. Never let fuel tanks overheat. Don't waste fuel; keep a stove turned to simmer. Practice lighting your own stove at home; each stove has a personality of its own. Refill your stove before it runs out of gas.

Fast, one-pot meals are best. A glop of quick-cooking ingredients tastes great after a long day. Add margarine or oil to dinners. Dry food has little fat and fat is the most concentrated form of energy. Don't diet on a ski tour. Your body is working hard and you will lose weight, even if you have seconds. On the other hand, don't bring so much food that your pack weighs an extra ten pounds. The only way to determine a menu is to count calories. On an overnight tour you could take a minimal amount of food, but on a longer trip, 2,500 to 4,000 calories per person per day are necessary.

Some skiers favor the Russian cosmonaut type of food. The story is that NASA feeds astronauts expensive and bland prepared foods, while the cosmonauts eat pastrami sandwiches and beer. Carry some easy to eat food which doesn't have to be cooked. Early explorers lived on pemmican, a mixture of fat and jerky, an optimum high energy food. We would have a difficult time trying to get by on a few pounds of pemmican every few days. It would take time for our system to adjust to such a concentrated diet. Use foods similar to those you eat at home. Peanut butter is an excellent food; a sort of vegetarian pemmican. Hard candies are nice when you're chugging up a pass.

Lots of liquid is important. Medical authorities think three or four quarts of water a day is necessary. Dehydration saps strength and causes nausea and headaches. Carry a *wide-mouth* water bottle and drink from it throughout the day. Keep filling it up with snow. In cold weather you may have to carry it near your body. Have it full when you go to bed at night; put your water bottle in your sleeping bag to keep it from freezing.

Cooking bannock
Photo: Sam King

## Day Tour Equipment List

Skis, shoes, poles

Mitts, hat, socks made of wool or similar material that will stay warm when wet.

Gaiters

Rain or storm shell or cagoule

Pocketknife with can opener

Waterproof matches, candles, butane lighter

Sunglasses, sunscreen

Toilet Paper

Rucksack or day pack

Map and compass

Flashlight

Wax

Lunch plus emergency food

First aid or emergency kit

Repair kit

Liter water bottle, full

**Optional Items:**

Extra sunglasses, mitts

Camera

Insoles

Magnifying glass for snow crystals

Thermometer

## Snow Camping Equipment List

Softpack with a good waistbelt

Sleeping bag, foam sleeping pad

Extra clothing, underwear, socks, bandana

PolarGuard booties

Parka or warm sweater

Spoon, bowl, insulated cup

Toiletries

Light windpants and shell

Snow shovel

Tent

Stove, fuel, pots

Food

**Optional Items:**

Camera

Book

Mukluks or overboots
Bivouac sack

Note: In steep terrain climbing skins are invaluable. Parties traveling in avalanche country must carry avalanche rescue beacons, probes and shovels. Without community gear your pack should not weigh over 25 pounds.

## First Aid Kit

High energy food
Cough drops
Space blanket, two or three for large groups
Flares
Water purifier (optional)
Waterproof matches
Candle
Pencil and paper—record details in an emergency
*Emergency First Aid* by Darvill—Lists necessary drugs.
Whistle
Tweezers
Moleskin, breathable surgical tape
Betadine ointment, aspirin
Wire splint
Bandaids, Telfa pads, suture strips, tweezers
Ace bandage, wire splint

Note: Inflatable plastic splints are useful on longer trips for broken bones to stop bleeding. Last person on tour should carry first aid and repair kits.

## Repair Kit

Combination slot and #3 Phillips screw driver
Small vise grips (the most used tool in your kit)
Strapping tape, duct tape
Five minute epoxy
Steel wool (insert in loose screw holes)
Dot rivets, wire
Nylon cord, at least seventy feet
Assorted screws
Ski binding parts (extra pin binding including bail)
Ski tip, ski pole baskets
Needle and thread, safety pins

Note: If your ski delaminates on a trip, use strapping tape or epoxy to repair it. For tears use duct tape, dot rivets, thread or safety pins.

Skiing in Giant Forest
Photo: Susan Beck

# Ski Technique

## Wax

Wax is intimidating. To listen to an old pro describe the day's wax, "I used a violet Fall Line base with a Rode green glider on my tip and tail and a wet Jackrabbit kicker," can make a beginner go right out and buy waxless skis. Don't let them scare you. Waxing doesn't have to be difficult.

Waxing skis requires time and wax skis require more dynamic technique. California snow, when it is near freezing, is hard to wax for; the wax you need can change from hour to hour. Manufacturers want to make skiing easy and pleasant; waxing can be a nuisance. That's why waxless skis were invented. They have many good qualities and for children, waxless skis are great.

Most people are undecided about skis; it's best to rent different types the first few times out. See what you prefer. Even if you are a confirmed waxless skier, try wax skis once in a while when the snow is cold and easy to wax for. It will help your technique. Remember, wax skis will glide and turn better than waxless skis. After a while you will find that waxing is fun and you will come to the magic morning when the wax is perfect and you seem to fly across meadows and over hills.

**Care of skis.** Plastic bases must be base waxed. The best wax to use for a base is either red alpine or glider wax. Base wax protects the base of the ski and binds the running wax. Skis with no base wax are slow, ice up, and the running wax wears off rapidly. If possible base wax waxless skis. If you can't iron in the wax, at least use a silicone spray on them. There are several liquid base waxes available which work well on waxless skis.

You should iron in a base wax. Put an old iron on the "wool" setting; an iron should never be so hot that wax smokes. Melt the wax by holding it on the iron as you move it over the ski. Dribble melted wax onto the base, then iron the wax into the

The wrong wax

base. When the ski cools, scrape the surface wax off with a metal scraper. The pores in the base will be full of wax. Repeat the melting-in process and scrape all but a thin film off with a plastic scraper.

Wood skis require a pine tar base. Spread a thin layer of the tar on the dry smooth wood base. Torch it until the tar just bubbles then quickly use a rag to wipe off the excess tar. When you ski, don't let the tar wear off. The wood will wear and get wet and the ski will not hold wax. In California, plastic bases work much better than wood. On ice or spring snow, a thin layer of green klister will work better than tar as a base wax. In Scandinavia where they don't have warm California snow, pine tar is the only wax many skiers use.

Running wax provides kick and glide. Apply a layer thick enough and soft enough so it will just grip when pushed into the snow. However, too much or too soft a wax and it will ice up. The layer must be thin enough and composed of a hard enough wax so that when pushed forward the ski will glide. There are many ways to achieve the balance between kick and glide. A thick layer of green will work like a thin layer of blue. Hard wax must be smoothed by a cork, thick spots will drag or ice up. Move the cork quickly and press moderately hard. Don't cork the layer away! Many thin layers are better than one thick layer.

Klister is sticky. Carry a rag and hand cleaner with you. To apply klister, spread a narrow strip on either side of the skis' groove along the kicker. Smooth it out with a scraper. In cold temperatures, you need a torch. On plastic skis, just wax the kicker strip, (the area a foot or so in front and to the rear of the binding).

Many skiers are using skins or climbers to climb long distances. Skins are strips of synthetic fur which you attach to the base of your ski. The Col-Tex system of attaching skins works best. Skins are quick to put on and off. They don't provide much glide but their grip is amazing. They allow you to climb the steepest slopes without ever slipping back. On multiday tours when you have a heavy pack, they're great.

# Wax Chart

| Snow Conditions | Air Temperature | °F | °C | Swix | Rex |
|---|---|---|---|---|---|
| **New Snow:** The original crystals are visible. Powder, Falling snow, Frost, Wild snow | Extreme cold: Snowball will not form | 5° | −15° | Polar −15°/− | Arctic −15°/−30° Turquoise −10°/− |
| | | 16° | −8° | Green Special −10°/−15° | Light Green −5/−10° |
| | Very cold: Snowball falls apart | 28° | −3° | Green −5°/−10° | Green −3/−5° |
| | Cold: Snowball forms | 32° | 0° | Blue −1°/−5° Blue Extra 0°/−2° | Blue −1°/−3° Blue Special −1°/−2° |
| | Transition: Firm snowball forms | 34° | 1° | Violet | Purple |
| | Damp: Snowball is hard | 35° | 2° | Red 0° damp Red Special 2°/1° | Red 2°/0° |
| | Wet: Water is visible | 41° | 5° | Yellow Klisterwax | Yellow 5°/0° |
| | Very wet: Rain | | | Yellow Klister | Red Klister Orange OI Klister |
| **Old Snow:** Snow that has never been melted, but the new-snow structure is not visible. Old powder, Old snow, Bonded snow, fine grained ET, TG snow | Extreme cold: | 14° | −10° | Green Special | Light Green −10°/− |
| | Very cold: | 20° | −7° | Green | Green |
| | Cold: | 30° | −1° | Blue Blue Extra | Blue −1°/−6° Blue Special |
| | Transition: | 34° | 1° | Violet | Purple |
| | Damp: | 35° | 2° | Red Red Special | Red |
| | Wet: | 41° | 5° | Yellow Klisterwax | Yellow |
| | Very wet: | | | Yellow Klister | Red Klister Orange OI Klister |
| **Corn Snow:** Snow that has been melted. Spring snow, Slush, Ice, skare, MF snow | Ice | 30° | −1° | Green Klister Blue Klister | Blue Klister −5°/− |
| | Transition | 34° | 1° | Violet Klister | Purple +/−7° |
| | Damp | | | Red Klister | Red Klister |
| | Slush | | | Silver Klister | Silver Brown OV Klister |

## Waxing Tips

1. Don't waste time corking and fussing. Go try the wax.

2. Stick to one brand; all waxes are slightly different. In the chart, manufacturers' recommended temperature ranges are given in centigrade.

3. Always let skis cool to snow temperature. Warm skis will ice up.

4. Start with less wax than you think you need. It's easier to add more wax than to take it off.

5. Wax must be "skied in." At first hard wax is too slippery and klister too sticky.

6. If your skis are slow or ice up try thinning the layer of wax with a cork. Or, try removing wax and applying a harder wax. Rub the ice off with candle wax.

|------|------|---------|-------------|-----------|
| Green Special –8°/– | Special Green –10°/–30° | Cold Special | | Light Green |
| Green –5°/–10° | Green –2°/–10° | Green –7°/– | Silke #1 | Green |
| Blue –2°/–6° | Blue 0°/–2° Super Blue | Blue 0°/–10° | Blandingsfore #2 | Blue |
| Violet | Violet | Violet | Blandingsfore #2 | Purple |
| Red 2°/–2° | Red 2°/0° | Red 2°/0° | Klistervox #3 | Red |
| Yellow 4°/0° | Yellow 4°/1° | Yellow 3°/1° | Klistervox #3 | Yellow |
| Red Klister | Red Klister | To Kristal Klister | Vat Nysno Klister #10 | Red Klister |
| Green Special –12°/– | Special Green | Cold Special | | Light Green |
| Green –7°/–13° | Green –4°/–10° | Green | Silke #1 | Green |
| Blue –2°/–8° | Blue –2°/–6° Super Blue | Blue | Gront Klister #7 | Blue |
| Violet | Violet | Violet | Blandingsfore #2 Vat Klister #8 | Purple |
| Red 2°/–2° | Red | Red | Vat Klister #8 | Red |
| Yellow 4°/0° | Yellow 4°/1° | Yellow | Vat Klister #8 | Yellow |
| Red Klister | Red Klister | To Kristal Klister | | Red Klister |
| Blue Klister | Spec Blue Klister –4°/–12° Blue Klister 0°/–5° | Skarkristal Klister | Skarevox #4 | Blue Klister |
| Violet Klister | Violet Klister | Skarkristal Klister | Skareklister #9 | Purple Klister |
| Red Klister | Red Klister | To Kristal Klister med Tajara | Vat Klister #8 | Red Klister |
| Silver Klister Orange Klister | Silver Klister Nera Klister | | | |

7. Tractor Treads are a California wax innovation good for conditions where skis load up with snow when damp surface snow is pushed down into cold soft snow. Rub a layer of candle wax along the whole ski base. Then for grip apply thin bars of running wax across the kicker zone of your ski.

8. On cold, icy snow with patches of powder, apply a thin layer of klister. Let it freeze and then apply hard wax over it. The skis won't ice up in powder but will grip on ice.

9. The minimum wax kit: a two-wax system such as Swix or Jackrabbit, a candle, tubes of violet and red klister plus a cork and scraper.

# Basic Lesson

Nordic skiing is easy to learn; after a few hours of practice a beginner is ready to go on a tour. Unlike alpine skiers, the majority of cross country skiers need only a few lessons. There is no single best way to ski, but there are some methods that work better than others. Don't fall into the technique trap. You are skiing well when you get around efficiently and comfortably; you don't have to look like a racer.

Over the years we have given thousands of lessons in our ski school; so this section comes from years of experience teaching everything from beginning diagonal stride to expert nordic downhill technique. The lessons are designed to be used on the snow as you learn. There are two sections: one for beginners and one describing downhill techniques. There are also sections on wax and survival skiing containing information on how to travel in the winter even if you are not an advanced skier.

Study the text and illustrations carefully. Don't go too fast. Have a good time and master each technique at your own pace. Learning is easy if it's fun. The setting for your start on skis is important. Find a flat area, uncrowded and friendly looking. A packed ski trail and good skiing snow help immeasurably. It's easier to learn on tracks. A narrow oval track at least fifty meters long works best. Skis should be about six or eight inches apart for balance.

After you have read the wax section and have a feel for the right wax, put on your skis. Be sure your boots are attached to the bindings properly, pins in holes. When you kick your foot the ski should stay on. Your heels should be square on the ski; be sure there is a heel plate to keep your boot from sliding off the ski. Check to make sure your skis are on the right feet, the bindings are marked "right" and "left".

At first, keep skis flat on the ground; ankles should never be bent sideways. You can't slide on a ski unless it's flat. Everyone should go around the track a few times. Remember your feet are now six feet long. Relax. There is a saying, "If you're not falling, you're not learning." Some experts have fallen thousands of times. Don't worry, falling with nordic skis is much safer than with alpine skis. Fall with as much style as you can. Keep your skis together and fall to the uphill side. Once down, relax, getting up is work. Never fight the snow. Take time and think things out. If you fall with a pack take it off before you get up. Roll onto your back and put your skis into the air to untangle your legs. Place your skis parallel to each other and take your pole straps off. Be sure your skis are sideways on the hill and won't slide when you stand up. Hold the poles in the middle and push them flat against the snow. Position yourself directly over your skis, then stand up. Use your legs to lift yourself. Never try to pull yourself up with your poles.

**Diagonal Stride.** This is the essence of nordic skiing. Think of it in terms of kick and glide. The kick is a downward step or push with your foot flat. The kick should be quick, a late kick will push a ski backward. The feeling of a kick is similar to that of walking flatfooted on an icy sidewalk. If you don't push directly downward, your foot will slip.

When you step off your kicking ski, push your knee and foot forward onto the gliding ski. The more weight you can put directly over the center of the ski the better the glide. Many beginners walk on their skis, they neither kick or glide. The gliding sensation is not a natural one. You have to learn it and then practice until it becomes rhythmic. After you stop walking and get a feel for the glide you will often glide on both skis. Your weight should be on the front gliding ski. If it's difficult to get the feel for the glide, practice on a long downhill track.

For the first half hour or so, ski around the track without your poles; it's easier to get the feeling of the basic diagonal. Swing your arms like a pendulum, sing a little song, don't go fast. Learn to rely on your legs because they are much stronger

Diagonal Stride

Sierra Shuffle

than your arms. Ski smoothly and feel the tempo or rhythm.  Vary the tempo, try a longer glide, try a sprint. Imagine that you are on a fifty kilometer tour and you have forty kilometers to go. Economize energy. Every bit should contribute to your forward motion.

Now use your poles. Put your hand up through the strap. When you hold the pole, the strap is between the handle and your palm. Hold the pole loosely so your shoulders won't tense up. When you swing your arm forward plant the pole's basket back at an angle near your foot. Push on it while you glide. As in golf, follow through with your pole plant. Get as much push from the pole as possible. At the end of the pole plant, the pole should be held loosely between your palm and thumb so it will extend further backward.

**Sierra Shuffle.** Is a slow, relaxed diagonal stride. Skis are barely lifted from the snow and arms swing easily, they aren't lifted high. It's a good technique for an afternoon stroll or for skiing long distances.

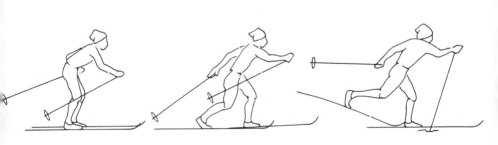

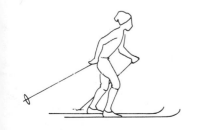

**Racing Stride.** Good skiers average over 10 miles per hour. A good kick and the extension of arms and legs maximizes glide. You swing both your shoulders and hips into the glide. Keep hands low and to the inside. It is literally running on skis. It takes several years to develop a good racing stride.

**Double Pole.** If you watch nordic racers you will see lots of double poling. Double poling is the fastest flat ski technique. Plant both poles out in front of you and as you push the pole back, bend your knees and shoulders forward, then stand up. Use your body and legs in addition to your arms. Some good double polers almost lunge forward. Novice skiers use the double pole on slight downhill slopes to get a little extra push. Kick when you double pole. You will feel as if you've been shot from a gun.

Double Pole

Uphill Diagonal

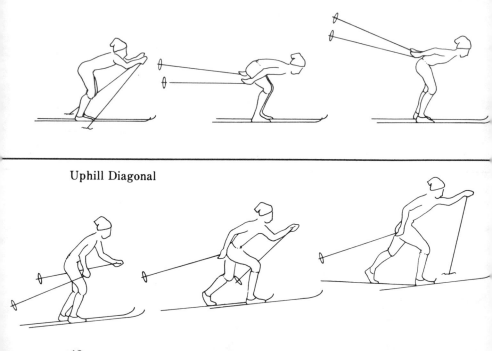

**Uphill Diagonal.** This is hard work. When you shift gears to  climb a hill, smooth technique helps. Your weight must be further forward, kick quicker and glide shorter. Never allow skis to slide backwards. At first jog uphill picking your skis up and slapping them into the snow for extra grip. Then smooth everything out. Make your skis glide uphill. Don't forget to push down and back with your poles, they will often make the extra difference.

**Herringbone.** As a hill gets steeper you will reach the point where you cannot diagonal stride up it. You must climb up on your edges. The herringbone is like an uphill duckwalk. Angle your knees inward so that your skis' inside edges bite into the snow. Your skis should form a V—rather like an inverted snowplow. Lean into the hill. Use your poles to help. Step each ski carefully, don't let your tails cross. Racers will even glide very slightly when they herringbone uphill. The herringbone is useful when you have to get up a short steep hill.

Herringbone

**Side Step.** The side step is another way to go up a hill. To side step be sure that your skis are at enough of an angle to the fall line so they won't slip. The fall line is the line directly downhill, the line a snowball would roll down. When you side step, the uphill edges of your skis bite into the snow. As you step uphill keep your feet flat on the skis. If you bend your knees slightly into the hill, the edges will have a better bite. It's easier to step uphill at an angle rather than simply stepping straight uphill with your skis sideways. Stay out of gullies or other places where you cannot use all of the skis' edges to climb. Side stepping is important in steep or narrow places where you can't traverse. Use your poles with each step; they will help your balance and give you that extra security.

**Schuss.** New skiers are often afraid of speed. They want to learn how to stop before they learn how to go. Most ski maneuvers are easier to perform with some speed. Schussing is easy. Climb to the top of a small hill and then ski directly down

Side Step

Schuss

it. Pick a packed slope and be sure that there is a good runout.  Always bend your knees—they are shock absorbers. Keep your upper arms close to your side with elbows slightly bent. Now push yourself off. Relax. Do a few gentle knee bends, try putting your hands on your knees. Don't sit back. In the schuss position your skis should be about eight inches apart. At times a schuss is the best way to come down a narrow trail. Keep schussing. It's fun and a good way to get used to speed. Never confuse speed with control. If you're in control you can stop and turn even if you are going fast.

Traverse. To traverse, ski across a slope rather than schuss down it. It requires more technique than schussing and it introduces the novice skier to weighting his skis. The downhill ski is weighted more, and the uphill ski is about six inches in front, acting as a feeler ski. Skis should be about six inches apart, knees are always bent into the hill and the upper body turned slightly downhill. Lead with the uphill shoulder and arm. Poles should be held slightly forward and ready to use. A stable traverse is essential. With your weight on the downhill ski, it's easy to use your uphill ski to step uphill when you want to turn or stop. You can ski down a steep hill by traversing across it. Step turn uphill to stop; do a kick turn and then traverse across in the opposite direction. Begin by taking a very slight angle and picking up just a little speed. Then it will be easy to stop, turn and repeat the exercise.

Traverse

**Kick Turn.** Several times a season we have beginning skiers who learn the kick turn while standing still and then ask how to do it when they're moving! You don't; it's a stationary turn. But it can be thrilling when you're doing one on top of a steep, icy couloir. The kick turn is essential to change direction on steep slopes or in confined areas.

With your skis, carefully pack a platform perpendicular to the fall line. Stand on the platform and turn your shoulders so you face downhill. Place both poles in the snow behind your skis, one behind the ski tips and one behind the ski tails. Form a stable tripod. Then kick your downhill ski forward and when your leg is extended, turn your ski around 180° and place it back on the platform. Now you're in an elementary ballet position. Relax. Bring the pole by your uphill ski around so that you are now facing the opposite direction. Then move your uphill ski around and place it next to your other ski. You will have completed a kick turn. Kick turns are a critical part of survival

Kick Turn

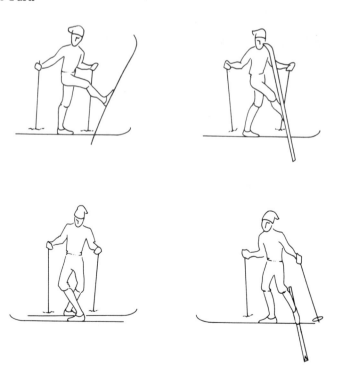

skiing. If you are on a hill and feel uneasy about skiing down,  kick turns and traverses work fine. You will get down without falling if you just take the time to do them right. One of the most challenging runs in California, KT-22 in Squaw Valley, was named because it took a skier twenty-two kick turns to get down.

**Snowplow.** The straight snowplow is an edged or skidded maneuver, handy on narrow trails and is a good way to check speed without turning. Find a slope where the snow has been packed down and as you schuss down the hill, bend your knees forward and push the tails of your skis apart. As you push your skis into a V position with the tips together, you will be able to feel the resistance to the snow as you push the inside edges of your skis out. Bend you knees slightly inward so that your inside edges skid down the hill.

To stop, push the tails of your skis further apart and use a little more edge. Be careful; if you apply too much edge a ski will stop skidding and run along its edge. "Catching an edge" is one of the first technical reasons you can give for falling. Like the kick turn and the traverse, the snowplow is a great way to come down a hill safely and in control; it is a good way to slow down.

Snowplow

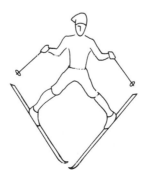

**Snowplow Turn.** After a successful snowplow, you are ready to snowplow turn. As you snowplow, rotate your body in the direction you wish to turn. Don't turn too much—you must turn from your knees; shoulders and hips turn as a unit. When you rotate, your weight will go onto your outside ski and you will turn. After a while you will find it easier to turn than to do a straight snowplow. A word of caution. The snowplow is a limited turn and is not very good in difficult snow conditions. Too many skiers try to snowplow in deep or soft snow and they invariably crash. They should use the step and telemark turns.

**Step Turn.** Many excellent Scandinavian skiers never learn more than the step turn; they step turn down the steepest runs. Novice skiers usually do only half a step, they don't follow through. They pick up one ski and place it in the new direction but they don't transfer their weight to it and the skis spread apart and they fall.

Pick a gentle hill. Start down with skis parallel. When you get to the bottom, simply pick up your skis, one at a time and step in the direction you want to go. If you want to turn left, pick up

Snowplow Turn

46

your left ski, point it in a left direction, transfer your weight to  it and quickly follow with the right ski. Both hands should be at your side pointed in the direction you want to go. Keep stepping around, transferring your weight, until you complete the turn. Short quick steps are best. Push with your poles, they help maintain speed and balance. Step turns are used all the time in skiing. You will always be stepping out of the way of something, or someone, or changing directions. A quick step is the best way to recover your balance.

**Skate Turn.** Skating on skis is the same as with ice skates. Edge a ski and push off it and glide on your other ski. Use poles for extra push and balance. Skating is the only accelerating turn, all others check rather than increase speed. It's useful when you must turn quickly. When wax isn't working, skating will grip the snow. Skate with no poles; it will help your arm motions and your balance. Use a large flat area with a hard surface to practice. Use your poles as in double poling. Try a forceful skate. Bend your knee and push hard off the ski's edge. Get a good glide. Skating is a great balance exercise. It's possible to skate uphill, downhill or on the level.

Skate Turn

Step Turn

Northside of Forester Pass

# Downhill Nordic Lesson

Many Californians who have been nordic skiing for a few seasons want more of a challenge. If you plan on wandering into the high country or want to ski downhill you will need to practice the following techniques.

**Telemark.** There are several advantages to the telemark. In soft or junk snow it's stable; a handy feature when skiing with a pack. It enables a skier to shift weight either forward or backward so that transitions such as snowdrifts, icy spots, bumps, gullies or changes of slope can be handled without a painful nose dive or a sudden sitz. Telemarks don't work well on very hard snow or ice. Expert skiers don't need to telemark, except in unusual circumstances, advanced parallel technique works better.

**Straight Running Telemark.** This position is not a turn, although once you learn it, the turn becomes easier. When you come to a transition in terrain, push one ski about a foot in front of the other. Weight both skis equally. When thrown forward, you will have the front ski to shift your weight onto; if thrown back, rock onto the rear ski. Keep your front foot flat on the ski and your knee bent forward. Bend your rear knee and lift your rear heel off the ski if necessary. Skis should be about eight inches apart. Never lean forward from the waist; the proper body position is similar to a deep knee bend. Keep your hands shoulder high, or lower and out to the side, ready for use. If you start to fall, use your poles to regain balance. Try a small jump and land in the telemark; jumpers in Norway invented the telemark in the last century. After a little practice you will find that instead of being thrown off balance by bumps and gullies, you can use them to maintain momentum.

---

Straight Running Telemark

## Telemark Turn

**Carved Telemark Turn.** When snow is deep, wet or crusty, you  must carve turns. Skidded turns, such as a snowplow, don't work. The tracks made by a carved telemark are narrow at the outside of the turn because the rear ski follows the front one; just the opposite to most turns, which look as though they were made with a windshield wiper.

To telemark to the right, advance the left ski, weight it and turn it to the right. Bend your left knee slightly inward, banking the ski in the direction of the turn. The inside edge of your front ski will carve the snow and you will turn along the arc of the two skis. A stable tripod is formed if you place the tip of your right ski against the toe of your left shoe. The telemark is the only turn where it is proper to cross your skis. The upper body position is the same as in the straight running telemark; front knee bent forward, rear knee low, front foot flat, rear foot with raised heel. You can help the turn by rotating your upper body in the direction you are turning. The carved telemark may take time to master but it's worth it. Some avid high-speed deep-powder telemarkers crouch very low with the tip of their rear ski against the heel of their front shoe. They even drag their rear knee in the snow below their rear ski, using it as a brake and to throw up snowplumes. Needless to say, if the rear ski slips behind the front shoe, the skier has a problem.

**Skidded Telemark Turn.** If you practice your telemarks on packed or hard snow, your edges may slide or skid out from under you. To practice a skidded telemark, choose a packed hill. Initiate the turn in the same manner as you would a carved telemark. As you go into the turn, increase the angle of the skis to each other, even to right angles, and lean inwards. Both uphill edges should slip or skid over the snow. Skis should be weighted more equally than in the carved telemark. It is a quick, neat turn and a fun way to end a downhill run.

**Stem Turn.** There are different forces involved in turning a pair of skis. Some of them have already been mentioned — when you rotate your body in the direction you want to go, your skis will turn. Point your knees in the direction you wish to turn; your skis will then tilt or rock onto their edges and slide along the arc of their sidecut. Sidecut refers to the shape of the ski; it

Stem Turn

is narrower in the middle and wider at the tip and tail. A ski with a soft flex will be easier to turn in soft snow or over bumps.

A stem turn begins with a snowplow turn. At the outside of the turn, when your skis are pointing downhill, weight your downhill or outside ski and bring your inside or uphill ski next to it. Most of your weight is on the downhill ski and both skis should be slipping sideways over the snow, skidding on their uphill edges. Don't edge your skis too much, push down with your heel. Bend your knees uphill and the skis' edges will catch the snow and you will skid to a stop in the traverse position. Be sure your upper body is facing in the direction you are going. Never lead with your lower arm. If anything, your upper shoulder should be slightly advanced and your upper arm leading. Repeat the stem until you feel comfortable. Then congratulations! Not only have you learned to stem but you have also learned to christie. You christie when you complete the stem turn; skis are parallel as you skid to a stop.

**Side-Slip.** Edge control is essential to advanced skiers. Now that you have the feeling of your edges, practice side-slipping; it works best if you have some speed. Get on a packed hill and practice traversing. Bend your knees uphill, set your edges and release them, letting the ski be flat on the hill; without the edges holding, the skis will slip downhill. You will end up skiing downhill at an angle. Side-slipping is quick and efficient; you can get down hills faster than if you were simply traversing. In narrow places where you can't turn, side-slipping is the only way to get down. It is important because it is a key to advanced skiing. When traversing, side-slip your skis just before a turn, you check your speed and can turn easier. Side-slipping will slow you down. Find some bumps and practice slipping and stemming over them.

Side-Slip

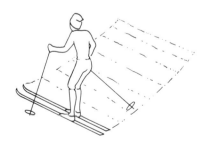

**Parallel Turn.** Ski over a bump and when the tips and tails of your skis are in the air rotate your body, rock your knees so that you change edges. Side-slip down the lower side of the bump. You have just performed a parallel turn. In addition to rotation and edging you have to unweight skis to parallel turn. In the stem you unweight when you step onto your new downhill ski. On a bump, use the terrain to unweight your skis. There are many ways to unweight skis. You may retract your knees to unweight. One classic way is to extend your knees as you plant your inside pole to initiate a turn. Unweight by lifting your upper body as you turn. Be aware which ski most of your weight is on. As you become a better skier you will be able to feel subtle differences in edging and weighting. In soft, deep powder, skiers unweight by lifting their arms and shoulders; while their skies are unweighted, they change edges and transfer a portion of their weight to their new outside or downhill ski. Since they often ski in bottomless snow, powder skiers tend to use both skis as a single unit; they often have their knees and boots touching. Other downhill technique requires a wider stance. Skiers on nordic skis will do best with a stance of

Parallel Turn

eight to twelve inches. Skiers in powder, breakable crust or soft snow cannot side-slip their skis. They must carve turns.

**Two-Pole Turn.** Some alpine skiers have pushed alpine skiing limits to what is called extreme skiing. Skiing the U-Notch in the Palisades or from the summit of the Grand Teton are examples. Elderberry Canyon, a 7,000 foot descent off the summit of Mount Tom is an example of extreme skiing. This skiing calls for superb edge control. The two-pole hop turn is standard for skiing steep terrain. For a tight turn, side-slip and christie almost to a stop. Plant the uphill pole near the uphill ski tip and the downhill pole to the rear. Unweighting doesn't come from pole plants; unweight by a quick edge set and then an easy hop against the edges into the fall line. Quickly christie to another edge set. If you set your edges well you spring up using little arm power. One doesn't really have to use both poles to turn. The two-pole turn is also handy for nordic skiers. On very steep slopes you cannot stop. Either you turn or fall all the way to the bottom. The limits of extreme skiing are pushed further every year. Experts are skiing slopes that they need ropes, ice axes and crampons to get to.

Two-Pole Turn

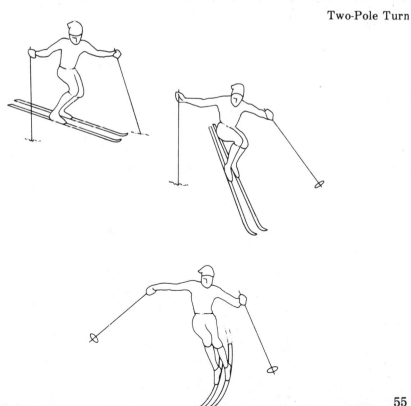

East side of Triple Divide Peak

## Survival Ski Technique

Nothing compares to being on top of Milestone Pass looking east to Mount Whitney and west toward the Great Western Divide. But it's hard work getting there. Climbing up the pass you'll feel tired, thirsty and probably discouraged. But your reward, in addition to the spectacular view, will be to link telemarks three miles down Milestone basin. When you're skiing in California corn snow, all the frustration is worth it. The following information, gleaned from years of experience and sore muscles will make ascents and descents a little easier.

Some people seem to muddle through; often they are not the best skiers with the most up-to-date equipment but sometimes they are the happiest. They seem to care more than others. If you don't try to achieve a ski touring goal, all the strength, skill and equipment won't help. One thing experienced skiers all agree on: mental attitude and effort are the most important aspects of skiing; whether it's racing, touring or ski mountaineering.

Some skiers tense up. Lack of confidence at the top of a steep slope is a common source of fear. Knowledge can overcome many fears. Learn to read the snow. Route finding is critical. Learn to carefully pick routes that will save time and energy. You are unlikely to hurt yourself if you fall, but repeatedly getting up, especially with a heavy pack, is exhausting. Falling is to be avoided. Ski conservatively. A confident traverse and kick turn is much more effective than a half-hearted carved telemark. Don't be afraid to walk. On steep hills, walking up or down is often the quickest way. Always wear safety straps in mountainous terrain. A lost ski could be a serious problem.

Get used to skiing downhill. Go to a ski area and practice skiing downhill on nordic skis. Learn what is possible on skis. With experience you will acquire a steadiness that has little to do with technique. You may never learn to parallel ski and your telemark may be minimal, but if you feel steady and comfortable on snow, you will do fine. Learn the kick turn and traverse then you can ski anywhere. The more you ski the more you learn the nuances of balance.

When skiing in the backcountry, don't take chances. There are always easier ways to get around. Never fight the snow. On most ski tours there is no ski patrol nearby. Ski cautiously when there is thirty miles between you and the nearest help.

Learn the straight running telemark. It is great for skiing through transitional snow, dips, and over bumps. Bend your knees; the more bumps you can absorb with your knees, the less you will fall.

## Uphill Pole Drag

## Pole Arrest

## Pole Drag

**Use your poles to help you on steep hills.** *Never* use pole straps  on steep hills or in brush or timber. It's better to go back for a ski pole rather than dislocate a shoulder. When traversing and side-slipping down a steep hill, hold both poles together. Put one hand near the baskets and one up by the handles, like you would hold a broom. Drag your ski poles in the snow on the uphill side. They will slow you down, give you control, and prepare you for a ski pole arrest if you fall. A ski pole arrest can prevent a long fall down an icy slope. If you fall, immediately jab your poles into the snow. The pole tips will dig into the hard snow and stop you from sliding. Practice the pole arrest until it becomes automatic.

Sit with your poles between your legs and slide down the hill using your poles as a brake. Sit near the baskets so as not to break the poles. This is a good technique to use if a hill is narrow and you can't turn or side-slip.

On a tour it's important that your group pace themselves. Carefully pick a route that everyone can ski. If there is a spot where it takes someone five minutes to get up from a fall and everyone falls, you will lose time. Avoid areas where your group may have to wait for each other. People will get cold standing in the snow. Skiers should not waste time. It's impolite to poke around adjusting packs and clothing while keeping everyone else waiting. Be ready; don't have your sunglasses at the bottom of your pack. *It is essential to always stay in sight of each other.* Never split a party up unnecessarily. Survival skiing is an important concept. Understanding it will help you both physically and mentally.

Storm front moving
in over San Joaquin River
Yosemite Trans-Sierra

# Environment

## Climate and Weather

In California mountains, the first snow generally falls in September but skiing doesn't usually begin until around Thanksgiving. The main controls for our winter storms are high-pressure areas in the Pacific, the Great Basin and the Pacific Northwest. In early winter, the Pacific high slowly drifts south following the sun, and storms follow it. In the northern part of California, December is the wettest month; in the south, February is. Official records do not confirm this observation, but it always seems that several consecutive weeks of clear weather occur during January or February. Perhaps the reason is the Great Basin high, once established, often lasts for several weeks, blocking storms from the Pacific.

If there is a high over the Pacific Northwest, storms originating in the Gulf of Alaska move south until the Pacific high diverts them eastward to California. These storms — called Hawaiian storms — are warm, and they bring large amounts of snow. California's more typical winter storms follow a more direct route from the Gulf of Alaska, moving southeast over northern California. These cold storms don't often reach the southern part of the state. The high over the Great Basin blocks some storms, diverting them from California. The Great Basin high also protects the state from storms from the northeast; only once every decade or so does a cold windy norther break through. Usually a warm maritime climate prevails in California, but winter in the Sierra is warm only in comparison to the severe winters elsewhere.

Mountain Weather. Since most ski touring country in California is mountainous, mountain weather processes, as well as the usual frontal ones, influence storms. As a storm is lifted over a mountain range, it cools, and cool air can hold less moisture. Consequently the windward side of a mountain (usually the west side of California) always has more precipitation than surrounding areas. In the Sierra, the greatest precipitation falls between 5000′ and 7000′ on the west slope, but the higher elevations hold the snow they do receive longer. A mountain can generate a storm when the surrounding country is sunny. As damp air is lifted over Mount Shasta a cloud cap forms over the peak and snow may fall. A mountain range with more varied topography than Mount Shasta has a more complex local weather system. The snow depths on the leeward sides of mountains can vary. One canyon on the east side of the Sierra may have 12 feet of snow while a few miles away there is almost no snow.

Chinooks. As a moist mass of air is lifted, it cools at the wet adiabatic rate, typically about 3°F every thousand feet. In perfectly dry ascending air, the cooling rate is 5.5°F per thousand feet. A descending air mass warms at the same rates. A chinook or foehn is a warm wind that occurs when dry air descends a mountain. Consider a storm that started at sea level at a temperature of 30° and then dropped to 0° and lost its moisture as it crossed a 10,000′ mountain crest. Warming at the dry rate it will be a warm 55° chinook by the time it reaches sea level at the leeward side of the range. Since California has a generally warm climate with warm days, chinooks here are not as obvious as in colder regions. When a high forms over the Great Basin, a dry wind blows outward from it. Part of this wind crosses the main Sierra crest as an east wind. The wind is usually cold, and often lasts for several days after a storm.

The Santa Ana is a dry, sometimes hot, wind common in southern California mountains. A Santa Ana is the same as the east wind; it is warmer and drier because of the lower elevations. The wind descends from the Great Basin, warming at the dry adiabatic rate. Intense Santa Anas have melted the southern California snowpack and brought an abrupt end to the touring season. This wind is particularly strong along the low passes in the southern mountains.

Valley winds occur on mountain slopes. During the day, when the lowlands are warm, the air heats up and warm air always moves uphill. At night in the higher elevations, the surface cools the air next to it and cold air always flows downhill. A valley wind will follow the same drainage pattern as water. In mountain areas where there is a large vertical relief, valley winds are stronger and more persistent and the night wind is cold and damp. Don't camp where such winds can blow. A lack of wind or unusual behavior of the wind is a sign that a change in the weather may be coming. A wind blowing uphill at night, if from the west, is a storm sign.

Forecasting Storms. It can be difficult to forecast a storm during a tour. The surest sign that a storm is nearing are sudden changes in wind direction followed by gusts from almost every direction. In California, it is unusual for a storm to originate in the east. Often what appears to be an eastern blizzard will be the tag end of a Pacific storm being blown back by an east wind.

Clouds are not always reliable indicators of storms. However, cirrus clouds (high, thin, icy clouds) are often followed by a storm in a few days. Dark, low rolling clouds mean that a storm is almost upon you. When you see them, expect to be skiing in new snow or rain. Some storms seem to blow up from nowhere. The best indicators of storms are the Weather Service forecasts. Weather forecasts for one or two days ahead are accurate. Longer range forecasts are less accurate but they give an idea of what kind of touring weather to expect.

Sundogs (rings around the sun) and moondogs (rings around the moon) are storm signs. When a storm is coming it pushes existing air masses in front of it so if you see smog flowing over mountain passes, you know that air is moving.

## Reading the Snow

Learning to read snow, to understand the moods of the winter environment, will increase your enjoyment of skiing and other winter sports. It is like the art of a river tourer who reads the water of a rapid — the swirls and eddies give clues to what is happening below the surface. The study of snow is complex. Jargon and confusing technical terms make learning how to read the snow difficult. Skiers often call snow by the wax they are using: green snow, yellow klister snow. There are special words and concepts about snow unfamiliar to us. Eskimos have a vast snow vocabulary. Snow rangers or members of avalanche control teams use a precise snow terminology mostly borrowed from the Swiss. The Avalanche Research Institute at Davos, Switzerland has been a source of snow information for years.

Wherever you go skiing in California you are likely to see signs of snow surveyors: ski or snowcat tracks, old trail markers or even a snow course. There are hundreds of snow measuring devices in the state. Some of them are markers that can be read from an airplane, others electronically communicate snow weight by the deformation of a giant rubber pillow. A typical snow course will be X-shaped and consist of ten or more spots where core samples are taken with a Mount Rose snow tube. The samples are weighed and the average water content is calculated. Don't ski on snow courses; it is impossible to get

Wind-sculpted snow

accurate measurements from a tracked course. The winter snowpack is a vast reservoir vital to the economic welfare of the state.

Most of the snow survey work is done by the United States Forest Service, the Park Service, and power company employees under the California Cooperative Snow Survey. The Department of Water Resources has only a few employees who do snow surveys themselves. Snow surveyors were some of the early ski touring pioneers spending many days in the high country skiing from snow course to snow course.

New Snow

Snow is constantly changing from the moment a snow crystal begins its existence in a fall storm cloud, to the warm afternoon in spring when the snowbank melts away. Snow changes both in the air and in the snowpack. A snow crystal begins when it forms around a small particle of dust, salt, or particulate smog. Not all crystals form into six-sided feathery crystals. The shape and size of the crystal depend on the temperature and humidity of the air around the crystal when it forms. Drier, colder conditions produce smaller simpler shapes. While the crystal is in the air it may be battered and broken by the wind or it may be blown through a cloud of cold water droplets where the crystal may become rimed. Rime occurs when super-cooled water droplets touch something solid and freeze. Trees and rocks exposed to storm winds are often covered with rime. Rimed crystals will occur in mountainous areas or anywhere there are turbulent winds.

Sometimes a snow crystal can be so covered with rime that it becomes a hollow pellet called graupel. Pellet snow will increase an avalanche hazard. Rimed new snow will require a thicker layer of wax because rime rounds the sharp points of a new snow crystal. You need a softer wax or a thicker layer of wax to get a proper kick.

Carry a small magnifying glass. Look at the crystals and grains of snow. With practice you can see what a snowpack is doing, what wax will be needed. On a cold clear winter evening you can ski along a stream or meadow and see brightly shining points of light floating down through the fading sun. Diamond dust or air hoar occurs when moist air is cooled past the point at which it cannot hold as much water vapor. Some of the vapor becomes tiny ice crystals. Hoar frost crystals form anywhere that moist air comes into contact with anything cold and solid; the snow surface, an aspen branch, or a tent wall. Remember, rime happens when liquid goes to solid and hoar when vapor goes to solid. During clear weather, layers of surface hoar will form in meadows and along streams. Surface hoar crystals look like small shingles pointing into the wind. A ski track covered with a thin coat of hoar frost is fast. When you ski through a thick layer of surface hoar you sometimes hear a faint tinkling sound as the crystals break.

There are all kinds of new snow. If it is cold, dry and there is no wind a very light loose powder called wild snow will fall. The wild snow crystals are not connected and they flow around each other. Wild snow is what powder skiers dream about. It billows and flows around your arms and legs as you float in it. You fly without wings. Unfortunately wild snow is rare; usually there is some bonding or connection between the new snow crystals. The wind, crystal type, warmth, or humidity cause crystals to bond together. Slightly bonded snow still offers excellent powder skiing. Look at pictures of powder skiers. Are their ski tracks sharp-edged and are there chunks of snow in the air around the skiers? If so, the snow is bonded. Are there gentle ripples from the wind on the snow surface? If so, the wind has bonded it. An important and fun skill is learning to read the snow.

Light reflected from the snow will tell you much. Are there bright sparkles from large crystals? New crystals will even sparkle in the light of a full moon. The dull glow from the rough surface of a new layer of cement snow will warn you of challenging skiing ahead. Damp or wet snow is well named Sierra cement. When the air is warm, near freezing or warmer, new snow crystals stick to each other as they fall. That's what a snowflake is; a conglomeration of falling snow crystals. When the flakes reach the snow surface they all bond together to form a cement layer. Skiing cement makes it difficult to snowplow or skid edges. Waxing is not easy. Cement is in between hard wax and klister. However, a heavy layer of cement does make a good base once it sets up. Wild snow and cement are two new snow extremes. Most new snow is somewhere in between.

# International Classification for Snow

Plate

Stellar Crystal

Column

Needle

Spatial Dendrite

Capped Column

Irregular Crystal

Graupel

Ice Pellet

Hail

## Old Snow

There are three basic ways in which snow on the ground changes or metamorphoses. They are: Equitemperature Metamorphism (ET), Temperature Gradient Metamorphism (TG), and Melt-Freeze Metamorphism (MF). If you want to read snow you must understand how and when these changes take place.

**Equitemperature Metamorphism.** Most new snow crystals have sharp edges and points. However, a snow crystal will immediately begin to change from the moment it reaches the ground. If the snow layer isn't wet and if the temperature of the layer is constant, the crystal will become a small round grain. Each snow crystal is surrounded by water vapor. Molecules from the crystal are constantly going from ice to vapor and then back again. However, when the vapor goes back to a solid it doesn't reform in the place it came from. The general rule of ET is that ice from the tips or convex parts of the crystals will change into vapor and then change back into ice on the hollow or concave part of the crystal. The end result of ET is a layer of snow composed of fine grains. Wherever two of the grains touch they form a concave surface which will become filled by ice. So, a layer of ET snow is well bonded. You can recognize it because ski tracks will have sharp edges. Breaking trail is not difficult because you don't sink in deeply. When the grains become small a layer of ET snow will settle or shrink.

Settlement is easy to see. Settling snow will pull down tree branches; rocks and obstructions become outlined. As snow undergoes ET, waxing becomes easier. The best skiing is on old cold ET snow. It is always fast and it's easy to get a good kick. ET snow is called "old" or "settled" powder. Its surface is usually smooth except in places where the wind has evaporated it. ET snow appears bright from the reflection of the small round grains. New snow or surface hoar with larger crystals will sparkle more.

At times a rapid ET process called age-hardening occurs. The wind, or any other process which compacts snow, accelerates ET. As the crystals are ground up they are reduced in size and there are more points of contact where they can bond. As two crystals are ground together the heat of friction will melt a thin layer of water between them. The film will instantly freeze and the dense snow layer will set up and become hard. Age-hardening is sometimes very rapid. Avalanche debris, snow moved by a plow, snow blown by the wind into a slab, and snow in a ski track are all age-hardened. An igloo is strong because the snow in the chinks and the snow smoothed over it have been age-hardened. The wind will blow snow off windward slopes and form a cornice on the lee slopes. Cornices consist of age-hardened snow. They can be extremely dangerous.

**Temperature Gradient Metamorphism.** Snow is a good energy radiator. In fact the snow often cools air next to it. A snow surface protected from the sunlight or warm winds can be quite cold, especially in early winter. Since snow is a good insulator, the base of a snowpack will often be warmer than the snow above it as heat from the ground warms it. If there is a temperature difference, or a gradient, in the layer of snow, TG will take place. Instead of going from convex to concave surfaces as in ET, water vapor from a crystal will redeposit on colder snow crystals forming a step-sided, cup-shaped TG crystal. When you look at TG snow through a magnifying glass you can see little steps and facets. Fully developed TG snow is called depth hoar. Depth hoar crystals do not bond well to each other; they are like ball bearings. Avalanches slide well on TG layers. The more TG occurs, the weaker the snow layer becomes. A layer of TG snow doesn't settle much. If you have ever been out skiing when a snowpack suddenly gives way beneath your skis you have tried to ski on TG snow.

**Equitemperature Metamorphism**

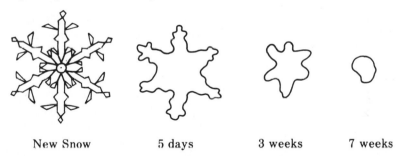

New Snow          5 days          3 weeks          7 weeks

**Temperature Gradient Metamorphism**

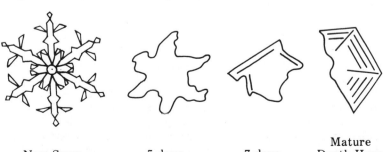

New Snow          5 days          7 days          Mature
                                                  Depth Hoar

69

As you climb higher into the mountains where the temperature drops five degrees with every thousand feet, you are more likely to find TG snow. In California we often get a TG layer if we have a few weeks of cold, clear weather. A TG layer poses an avalanche hazard if it becomes covered by a slab. Always poke around the snow with your ski pole; it's not too difficult to feel a buried TG layer. It's less resistant to your basket than other layers.

Suncups form on south slopes during long periods of clear weather. In the first part of the winter suncupped south slopes frequently indicate TG snow on colder slopes. No one knows why suncups form. However, any experienced skier knows how difficult, if not impossible, it is to ski on a knife-edged suncupped slope.

**Melt-Freeze Metamorphism.** No one likes to ski on breakable crust, which is a thin layer of ice over a soft layer of snow. A breakable crust is the first sign of melt-freeze metamorphism. In early winter the sun has a minimal effect on the snow. Days are short and the sun is low. About ninety percent of the light is reflected into the atmosphere. As the days get longer, more solar energy reaches the snowpack and a daily cycle becomes noticeable. The snow surface warms up and becomes wet during the day and then freezes into a breakable crust at night. At first only south slopes and other sunny slopes are affected, but as spring progresses MF becomes common. When MF first takes place the skiing is not fun. You are either on breakable crust or on fine grained wet snow. Have you ever tried to ski on snow that is wet on the surface but cold a few inches down? Every time your ski pushes the wet snow down into the cold snow it freezes and you end up with great lumps of snow sticking to the ski. Rub the lumps of snow off with candle wax. After the MF cycle repeats itself the skiing improves. Each day meltwater flows down through the pack and coats the grains with water which freeze at night. The grains get larger as they are repeatedly coated until they look like grains of corn, which is why spring snow is also called corn snow. In California we have excellent corn or spring skiing from March onward. Corn snow skiing is better in the regions which get a warmer, denser snowpack. Corn is one of the best snows for wilderness skiing. However, the two extremes of MF snow, ice and slush, certainly aren't. But when the corn has just begun to soften under the early morning sun you can ski anywhere and make linked turns down a slope. You don't have to pack a trail; that's why we do our extended ski tours in the spring.

If it rains or there is a warm wind, MF can take place anytime
during the winter. Snow saturated with water is very
dangerous—a sure avalanche hazard. Old corn or ice crusts
have a dull, white, sometimes transparent look to them. Wet
corn snow has a dull sheen. I have seen a ridge of corn snow
covered by a thin glaze of ice which looked as if it was on fire
with the setting sun. As water flows through snow it will form
channels which will be like a washboard when the pack freezes.
MF crust will often form under trees. One of the very practical
advantages to reading the snow is being able to anticipate and
avoid these icy spots.

It is possible for you to encounter all the different types of
snow on one tour. You start out on ET snow in age-hardened
tracks. Then you might ski on surface hoar along a stream.
Breaking trail up to a ridge would be more difficult because of
the deep TG. At the top you would avoid a large cornice and
carefully edge along a hard windswept MF surface caused by a
rainstorm a month before. You would hurry down; you don't
want to ski a south slope too late in the afternoon; wet corn
forms a breakable crust once the sun leaves it. When you begin
to understand snow other aspects of winter begin to make
sense. Reading the snow helps you select the right wax. It
helps you ski. It helps you avoid avalanches.

Suncupped snow
in the Upper Kern Canyon
Photo: Marshall Crossman

# Avalanches

Winter is the least forgiving of the seasons. The combination of cold, snow, wind and mountains can lead to tragedy. Cold is probably the most hazardous element. More winter travelers die from hypothermia (exposure) than in avalanches. Protection from cold is mostly a matter of common sense. Protection from avalanches is more difficult. They are seldom seen and the clues to their potential are obscure. Some winter travelers don't even believe in them. While they occur with great regularity in remote areas, until recently they were of little concern. Now avalanches are a concern as each winter skiers wander further into the mountains. Most avalanches occur during storms and the evidence they leave is quickly covered by falling and drifting snow. Avalanches don't last very long—a few minutes at most. There are probably more close calls than most people realize; skiers miss them by hours or even minutes.

Wilderness skiers are always asking about the avalanche hazard on their proposed tours. They want a yes or no answer to their question, "Are there going to be avalanches?" There are no easy answers. Avalanche forecasting is as much an art as a science. Snow conditions change rapidly in both time and place. While there may be safe skiing in one canyon, the snow conditions a few canyons away may be deadly. Be cautious and suspicious. If you wish to travel in avalanche country, study all you can find about snow, avalanches, route finding and then use that information to acquire experience. Skiers who get into trouble are often those with enough experience to travel into the mountains but not enough to avoid avalanches.

Avalanche probe line

Avalanche Paths. For an avalanche to occur, there must be an avalanche path. Wet snow avalanches have happened on slopes of only ten degrees but most avalanches need slopes over twenty-five degrees. Very steep slopes tend to have many small avalanches called sluffs. Avalanches must have a sliding surface: a smooth rock or a layer of snow. Rock outcrops or chaparral ten feet high will anchor up to ten feet of snow. A timbered slope will also anchor a snowpack. However, an avalanche sweeping through a stand of timber might not be big enough to harm the trees but could bury a skier.

New Snow Avalanches. Most avalanches occur during or just after storms. The snow that slides is usually new. New snow buildup is the most common cause or trigger of avalanches. There are many factors to consider when evaluating a new-snow avalanche hazard. How fast is the snow falling? Three inches an hour is a high snowfall rate in California. How long has the high rate lasted? If a snowlayer builds up faster than it settles, the hazard will increase.

When wild snow (loose snow with no crystal bonding) slides, a point avalanche occurs. Usually it's a small affair which originates from a single point and spreads out as it slides.

Most big avalanches start as slabs. When a slab lets go it slides as a single mass; it doesn't break up until after it has started to move. The most characteristic sign of a slab avalanche is the fracture line or crown it leaves. Most slab avalanches are associated with a weak layer of snow underneath the slab. Slabs are layers of age-hardened or settled snow usually created by the wind. Think of a slab as a stressed dome. It has strength enough to hold itself up, but the loading of more snow or the cutting action of a pair of skis can cause it to collapse and slide.

Wind transports snow. The lee sides of ridges always have a greater buildup of snow than the windward. A cornice is a large slab built up on the lee side of a ridge. Some cornices are big monsters to be avoided at all cost. A slab will often form below a cornice. Remember, slabs can form even if there is no new snow. Blowing and drifting snow will rapidly form a slab. Banners or plumes of blowing snow from high ridges and peaks are a sign of slab formation. There are other signs which warn of a slab: a weak buried layer, cracks shooting out in front of your skis, the slab collapsing making a "whumph" sound, fracture lines from recent slides. Poke the snow with your pole. Are there buried layers less resistant than the top layer? Find a small slope and test ski it. Does it collapse when you ski across it? Test slopes with different exposures.

Test skiing a hazardous slab

When rain falls on snow it often triggers a slide. As water soaks down through the top layers of the snowpack it adds  weight and melts the bonds between the crystals, literally ungluing the snowpack. Once wet snow freezes an ice layer forms; an excellent sliding surface for future avalanches. Once a slope avalanches it is smoothed out and irregularities are rounded and filled. The slope is apt to slide for the rest of the season.

**Old Snow Avalanches.** When there is a weak layer of TG snow covered by a stressed slab there is likely to be an avalanche. TG is more common in cold climates like Alaska or the Rockies. Take a thermometer with you on your tours; dig down into the snow and look for any temperature differences. Can you see any TG crystals under the magnifying glass? Look for facets or flat crystal faces. Are some layers of snow weaker than others? Find out. Push your mitts or a pencil into the layers and test their strength. In ski resorts on National Forest land snow rangers determine avalanche conditions. In addition to checking the surface snow, they dig pits every week or so. They look for layers such as old TG, buried MF ice crusts or wet snow.

In spring the snow warms up and meltwater begins to flow through the pack just like rain during a storm. If the water flowing down hits an impermeable layer such as ice, it will flow along and lubricate it, undermining the snow above it. In California there are a few nights in early spring when there is a warm spell and it doesn't freeze at night. The weather is balmy and everyone gets sunburned skiing in shorts. The freeze half of the MF cycle isn't working and meltwater is reaching down to the bottom of the snowpack for the first time where there may be TG or MF snow. Spring avalanches may result. Whole mountainsides of snow can slide. Forests in the path of the flowing snow can be wiped out. A cold night when the temperature is at least several degrees below freezing is a safe sign.

**Travel in Avalanche Country.** Someday you may make a mistake and find yourself in the awkward situation of skiing in avalanche terrain. The only safe way to ski across an avalanche path is along the ridge above it, often an impossibility. The worst place to cross a slide path is in the area where you might trigger the slide. Stay out of trigger zones. When you ski below the trigger zone you are still exposing your party to a risk. Narrow gullies are bad routes because just a little avalanche can pile up a lot of debris.

**If your party finds itself skiing in an avalanche path:**

* Space your party so that everyone is in sight of as many of the party members as possible.
* Use avalanche cords and be sure they are securely tied to you.
* Use avalanche rescue beacons. They are far more effective than the cords. They are expensive and take practice but they work. Practice finding a buried beacon.
* Do not use: safety straps or waistbelts. You may want to get rid of your gear in a hurry.
* Cross dangerous areas one at a time.
* If the snow is not too soft take your skis off and walk, straight up or down; you are less likely to cut a slab by walking.
* Take advantage of the terrain, ski between outcrops or trees.
* Avoid the steeper slopes.
* Wear warm clothing. Have food, matches, a hat and other emergency items you may need in your pockets in case you lose your pack.

We always carry snow shovels, rescue beacons and ski poles that make into probe poles. On a multi-day tour, we prefer at least four people in a tour party.

**If you are caught in an avalanche:**

* Try and ski out of it. If that is impossible, get rid of your poles, skis and pack.
* Swim. Some avalanche experts believe that the backstroke is best. Arch your back and stroke with your arms. Stay on top of the snow.
* When the slide begins to slow down, lunge upward. Reach up with one hand and spread your legs. An arm or leg may stick out of the debris. Use your other arm to create an air space around your face.
* Once stopped, debris instantly hardens. You won't be able to move. You may hear your rescuers but they won't hear you. *Relax, save oxygen.*

**Rescue.** According to the Forest Service fifty percent of the people buried in avalanches die within one hour. Rescue is up to your party. Don't wait for help. Of course, if you have a large party and help is near, send for it.

You must make several more difficult decisions:

* Is there a further avalanche hazard? Is the risk too great to try a rescue?
* Post an avalanche guard and have everyone stamp a route to escape another slide.
* Mark the point where the victim was last seen and quickly search from it in a fan-shaped area spreading out and downward. Scuff the snow and probe likely burial sites: in front of trees or rocks, below cliffs, on the outside of turns and in areas where the debris has piled up. Whenever you find anything belonging to the victim, mark its location: it may be possible to determine where the victim was carried.
* If drifting or falling snow or tramping might obscure the debris, mark the area so you will know where to probe. Hurry!

Probing. Line everyone up below a likely area and have them stand arms outstretched, fingertip to fingertip. Move quickly but carefully. The coarse probe is on a two-and-a-half foot square grid. Fine probing, on a one-foot grid, is less likely to locate a buried skier in time. A string or rope will help maintain the line. Probers' feet should be about two and-a-half feet apart. The probe leader commands "probe right" and everybody probes by their right toe. The leader looks along the tops of the probes to see if one is high. The leader then commands "probe left" and everyone withdraws their probes and probes by their left toe. The two rescuers at either end of the line then advance the string two-and-a-half feet forward. At the command "probe right" everyone withdraws their probes and advances to the new line and probes by their right toe. Probing isn't a very fast way of searching an avalanche but without a cord or beacon it's the only way. Trained dogs are good at finding people but they are usually not available. When you find the victim apply cardio-pulmonary resuscitation if necessary. The American Red Cross has an excellent CPR course. Assume the victim has injuries, possibly broken bones.

Few people die in avalanches when compared to the number of ski tourers. However, if you are on top of a pass you want to do everything not to become one of the few. Learn to read and understand the snow. The more trips you take, the more you read on the subject, the more experienced you'll become.

A cornice

## Route Finding

Route finding is the finest art of wilderness skiing. A back-country skier must be able to read the snow, the mountains and the sky for a safe and pleasant tour. There are times when a tour party must be skiing by sunrise to get over a pass before a storm closes in. There are times when an experienced wilderness skier will refuse to travel if there is an avalanche hazard. It is hard to turn back from a tour when the weather is sunny and half the party doesn't want to believe there is any avalanche hazard. But you only have to be wrong once.

Always check with a nearby ranger station or ski patrol to see whether any avalanche danger exists. Remember that snow can change quickly; a safe slope can become dangerous in a few hours. Always check the weather forecast for storms. On a long tour, plot several safe alternate routes out.

**Knowledge of landforms is useful.** It helps you anticipate the shape of the terrain. In a glaciated granitic canyon, expect a series of stepped cliffs and hanging valleys. A hanging valley is the product of glaciers; the glacier in the main valley carved a deeper canyon than the glaciers in the tributary canyons. The result is that the mouth of a tributary canyon is above the floor of the main canyon and the tributary valley is "hanging."

In non-granitic regions slopes are smoother but deep ravines at the mouths of valleys are more common. A steep-sided ravine is difficult and dangerous to ski in. The steep sides might avalanche and in a narrow ravine even a small avalanche can bury a skier under many feet of snow. Always look for a shelf above a ravine. At the head of a glaciated canyon there is almost always an amphitheaterlike *cirque*. The steep divide between two cirques is an *arete*. A *col* is a notch in an arete. Usually below a col there is a steep, narrow chute or *couloir*. The best routes in mountainous terrain often lead over passes or gaps.

Cornices are common avalanche triggers and are very dangerous. When skiing near one, stay at least twice as far from a cornice lip as you think necessary. There is no safe way across a cornice, particularly if it is soft. If you cross a small one, take off your skis and walk directly across it at a right angle to the ridge. Use a rope if there is any possible hazard. Immediately below the leeward side of a cornice, a snow pillow will form. Pillows are often dangerous to ski on; they are wind slabs. Snow builds up on them very quickly and they are usually in the shade where snow doesn't settle rapidly. At times a change in wind will conceal a cornice by filling the space beneath it with snow, but if the wind blows hard enough and long enough it will completely remove a cornice.

Snow Bridges across streams can be dangerous. Often you have to ski some distance along a creek before you find a snow bridge that will support you. Probe a bridge with your pole; new and wet snow form weak bridges. If your pole goes through, don't cross there. On a steep slope if a stream disappears into a hole in a snowpack, watch out, it might be the top of a waterfall.

In late spring when the snow is very wet and melting rapidly, skiing slopes with large boulders is difficult. The snow has melted around the rocks, forming hidden hollows. Falling into such a hollow is similar to falling into a crevasse in a glacier; it can cause a serious injury. The hollows can be ten to fifteen feet deep and are common in April and May in the high Sierra. High wind will scoop wind hollows around trees. The hollows may be covered by new snow and create another crevasse-like hazard.

There is often open water near inlets and outlets of lakes. Never trust lake ice — you need at least four inches for it to be safe. As the snowpack builds up through the winter it will settle into the lake water. There will be alternate layers of ice and saturated snow floating on a lake. Some of the ice layers may be melted away. In early winter or early spring, be careful, probe with your pole to see if you're on ice or just wet snow.

Plateau

Saddle

Avalanche Path

Hanging Valley

Ravine

U-Shaped Valley

# Geographical Features
# Related to Route Finding

Horn

Arete

Col

Cirque

Couloir

Tarn

Moraine-Dammed Lake

Moraine

Ground cover will influence route selection. For example, a good late-season route may be impassable during early winter because of chaparral or small cliffs. When you tour in dense timber, consult your compass and map often. Be careful when crossing timbered ridges; it is very easy to ski down the wrong slope and become lost, or at least lose time climbing back to the correct route. All members of a touring party should stay within sight of one another. It is easy to get lost particularly when skiing downhill. *Every tour party should have a sweep; a person assigned to bring up the rear.*

**Map and Compass.** Nobody intends to get lost but there are few tourers who have not lost their way at least once. More than one experienced skier has become lost on an easy, one-hour tour. Even where there are prominent peaks as landmarks, skiers can become disoriented if they ski in dense timber, are caught in a storm or if night falls. Navigational aids such as trails, signs and streams can be completely obscured by snow. Always carry a map and compass and know how to use them. If not, expect to bivouac.

Orienteering is a popular game in Scandinavian countries. A competitor uses a map and compass to find a route that passes six or more established points. He or she may follow contours and utilize geographical features, or they may follow a direct "beeline." An orienteering game is fun and the best way to get actual on-the-scene navigation experience.

True north marks the North Pole, the geographical top of the world. A compass needle points to magnetic north. In California magnetic north is declined from 15° to 20° east of true north. For example, in Mammoth, magnetic north is 17° to the right of true north. On most maps true north is at the top but always check. Be sure you are reading your compass correctly, on some compasses south is mistaken for north. Skiers sometimes draw in magnetic north lines on their maps. Use your compass to determine the direction of a meadow or road and test your reckoning. Follow the course. It's important that you trust your compass and your ability to navigate.

In steep areas an altimeter is helpful. You may follow a compass course to an elevation and then change directions to a new elevation. With an altimeter and compass it's possible to navigate completely without landmarks.

Topographic Maps. For general use the United States Geologic
Survey topographic 15 minute quadrangle maps are best. Each
map covers an area 15 minutes in latitude by 15 minutes in
longitude. It shows natural and whatever man-made features
existed when the area was surveyed. It shows landforms by
means of contour lines printed in brown. A contour line passes
through points of equal elevation. The contour interval on 15
minute topo maps is usually 80 feet. Within an 80 foot contour
interval there may be a 70 foot cliff that the map doesn't show.
The scale on most 15 minute topos is 1:62500. One inch on the
map represents about one mile of horizontal distance.
Timbered areas on topos are shown in solid green; brush or
chaparral by green dots. The boundary of a green area may be
only approximate. An area that is green on the map may in
reality be very thinly timbered and another area with thin
timber may not be shown in green at all. Many meadows are
shown larger than they really are. The contour lines in forests
are not as accurate as in open areas.

Practice matching features on the map with the landforms
they represent. Stop where there is a good view, orient the
map with your compass and identify the landmarks.
Remember that the distances between contour lines indicate
slope; the closer together the contour lines, the steeper the
slope. At first, your sense of scale may be way off; you will
mistake a mountain ten miles away for one only five miles
away. Practice with a topo map; in addition to being fun, it
could save your life. Get into the habit of consulting your map
often.

**If you get lost.** Perhaps all you will need is a thoughtful consultation with map and compass. Never split your party up, never panic. If you think you might be lost, be sure you don't wander on and become more lost. When you travel through timber or during a storm, check your compass periodically to be sure you are not skiing in a circle. Distances can be hard to estimate on skis. What seems a mile during a storm or at twilight may be only a hundred yards the next morning when the sun is out.

If you know the area where you're lost is bordered by a hard-to-miss feature like a river, a highway, a telephone line, follow a compass course to it. In timber it is easy to cross a low ridge without realizing it, so if your destination is downhill don't assume you are on course just because you're skiing downhill. It may be the wrong hill. In other parts of the country people are advised, if lost, to ski downstream. In California this advice could lead you to a cliff or result in having to bushwhack through miles of steep chaparral.

If you cannot find your way, make an emergency camp. Don't wait until it's dark or you're exhausted. Pick a prominent spot, a meadow or open ridge, make your presence as obvious as possible. To make search operations easier and more successful remain in one spot. Build a fire and a snowcave and wait. A touring party known to be missing in a remote area will be searched for by aircraft. Make a large sign in the snow for a plane or helicopter; three of anything is the universal signal for distress. A mirror makes a good signal. Aircraft fly high over mountains because of air turbulence so make the sign or signal as visible as possible. In rugged terrain you will probably be saved by helicopter, so stay in a large flat area where it can land. Never come close to a helicopter until the pilot tells you it's safe. Keep up everyone's spirits. Exercise to stay warm; build a warm fire and a seat of tree boughs, huddle together to stay warm. A snowhole near a bent-over tree is easy to build. Don't ever give up.

# Winter Wildlife

It is an unusual ski tour when you don't see animal tracks. Tracks are fascinating; they always tell a story. Sometimes it's a short story—a chickaree dashing out to harvest some nuts from a Jeffrey pine cone. Sometimes the story is hard to read, like the one told by the erratic, widely spaced tracks of a white-tailed jackrabbit as he dodges the pursuing coyote. Animal tracks are one of the nicest parts of ski touring and one of the benefits that you don't get from summer hiking.

**Coyote.** Coyotes are everywhere. Their tracks are found from the low desert to the highest mountain passes. The front paw print is larger than the rear one. You are more likely to see coyotes in the winter because they are so visible in the snow. Coyotes do not seem to be afraid of skiers, perhaps because they don't associate them with people. The large mountain coyote with its thick, dark coat is often mistaken for a dog or even a wolf. (By the way, there are no wolves in the Sierra.) Coyotes eat anything—juniper or manzanita berries, rabbits, mice, and carrion (animal carcasses) left from the hunting season. It is a true wilderness experience to be cozy in your tent on an overnight ski tour and hear the coyotes howl.

**Rabbit.** A motionless, white-tailed rabbit is almost invisible on snow. It can thus avoid predators such as coyotes. You probably won't see the rabbit until it takes off right in front of your ski tips. The snowshoe hare, which many skiers assume is the

Pine marten

only rabbit in snow country, doesn't range south of Lake Tahoe. The white-tailed rabbit does, but is rare in parts of its range. If you take the spacing and size of the tracks into account, the animal can often be identified. Snowshoe hare tracks are about one-third as big as the white-tailed rabbit.

**Mouse.** The little deer mouse is the most common mammal in California mountains. It spends most of its time under the snow, infrequently coming out to the surface. The meadow mouse, or vole, a near relative of the arctic lemming, also lives under the snow. It occasionally leaves its runways in the grass under the snow and ventures to the top. When the snow is shallow enough, predators dig down to the ground to hunt. A deer mouse's tracks are smaller than a meadow mouse's and they are arranged in a box shape. A vole's tracks are strung out in an irregular line. Unless the tracks are fresh, they are difficult to tell apart.

**Pine marten.** This is one of the chickaree's most effective predators. A marten climbs very well and captures its prey in the trees. When marten fur (sable) was very much in demand, the animal was extensively trapped. It has been protected since the late 1950's and its population has been slowly increasing. The marten's tracks are not too common. You have to look carefully to find them. You can expect to find marten tracks near those left by a chickaree.

Marmot hole in early spring

**Chickaree.** An energetic chickaree is often seen on a high pine branch scolding skiers who are passing under its realm. The chickaree is active year-round, harvesting seeds from pine and fir cones. You will often see this squirrel's web-like tracks leading from tree to tree. Look for tracks above 5000'.

**Weasel.** You will probably see the tracks of the weasel. This small predator is very active in winter. It often runs in leaps. Its tracks will often end abruptly, showing where the weasel burrowed into the snow hunting mice. Weasels are curious animals; sometimes you will find the tracks of one that has investigated your camp. If you ski along quietly and keep your eyes open you may see one.

**Wolverine.** Weasels and martens are members of the family Mustelidae. If you are fortunate, you may see the tracks of another, very rare mustelid, the wolverine. Once common throughout the Sierra, they are now rarely seen. You are most likely to see its tracks near the mountain passes in Sequoia National Park. The animal is so rare that no one knows its exact range or population.

**Bear.** During the first few weeks in April hungry bears come out of hibernation. Bears hibernate at fairly high elevations. When they emerge in the spring, they have to go down lower to find food. While they are still in snowy elevations, they will readily raid a skier's camp. After the first of April, be wary and bearproof your campsite. Tie your food in a bag and suspend it on a cord between two trees. It must be at least fifteen feet off the ground and six feet from the tree trunk. In soft snow a bear track is a deep trench.

**Porcupine.** Porcupine tracks (not pictured) look as if someone had dragged a broom across the snow as he walked along. The tracks are rare as the animal likes to stay in its tree. A porcupine tree is easy to spot: the bark is chewed off in large, irregular sections.

**Gopher.** Near the edges of melting snowbanks you will often see winding coils of soil on the ground. They are gopher cores made by pocket gophers. The gopher digs tunnels in the snow and then fills them with soil from his underground tunnels. When the snow melts a gopher core descends to the ground and is still in the shape of a thick, winding rope.

**Birds.** The most common bird that a skier will see in snow country is the chickadee. This sprightly little bird spends most of its time gleaning insects from pine branches. The Clark Nutcracker's loud call and bold behavior make it hard to overlook.

During the winter this camp robber will take any food that is offered. The dusky grouse lives in coniferous trees year-round, where it feeds on tender needles. Look for its droppings under tree boughs. The bird will often sit on the same limb long enough that its droppings become noticeable. In spring the male emits a very low rhythmic vibrato call to attract the female. Because the note is repeated at a rate similar to the human pulse, suggestible skiers have become convinced that they were hearing their own heartbeat.

**Insects and spiders.** Smaller life forms live in and on the snowpack. Some of the small insects and spiders you might see can be considered exotic because they are in the snow by accident—blown in by the wind. But others are right at home on the snow surface, and are well adapted to life in the cold. Look at the small spider hunting on the snow; his feet are insulated with hair and he always holds his body off the snow.

**Algae.** One of the most curious phenomena seen in the spring is pink snow. The pink color shows that a colony of algae is present in its resting state. During the active growing state, the minute plants are green. Green snow is rarer. You are most likely to see it early in the spring, or later in shady places. The little algae are motile; they swim up and down through the wet snow. On a bright, sunny day the algae swim below the snow surface. That is why ski tracks are sometimes deep pink on a light pink background. The ecology of the algae is not well known. It is likely that there is quite a complex ecosystem within a spring snowpack of which algae is an important part.

Wolverine tracks in
Kings Canyon

# Winter Animal Tracks

6″

Coyote

12″

White-Tailed Rabbit

1″

Deer Mouse

1″

Meadow Mouse

3″

Chickaree

**Pine Marten**

6″

**Weasel**

3″

**Wolverine**

12″

**Bear**

12″

At the end of
the Sierra High Route
Photo: John Bagley

# The Tours

The tours in this book are classified as nordic or alpine. For a nordic tour, light touring or touring skis are best; for the alpine tours, alpine or mountain skis are preferable. Experienced nordic skiers could ski most of the tours classified as alpine.

This guide describes at least one tour in each of the most popular touring areas in California. It is not so comprehensive that every tour in an area is included, for a large part of the fun of touring is finding and exploring new routes. This guide will take you on tours that will help you get a feel for different touring areas.

In the descriptions, vertical distances are in feet while horizontal distances are in miles. Metric equivalents are given in the tour headings. The tour maps are reproductions of 7 or 15 minute USGS topographic maps. There is a prominent North arrow. The single barbed arrow to the right of the North arrow points to magnetic north.

The symbols on the maps have the following meanings:

--~~~   described route
·······   alternate route
———   plowed road
▲   beginning of tour

When you park your car, guard against its being snowed in by a storm. It may be advisable for one member of your party to drive it to a lower elevation or at least to a spot near a highway that is plowed. Emergency brakes sometimes freeze tight, so it may be better to chock the wheels than use the brakes. Fill up your radiator with antifreeze and your engine with a low-weight oil; gas antifreeze will stop a small grain of ice from plugging a gas line. Most service stations in the mountains stock it. Batteries get weak quickly in cold weather; if possible, park your car where you can push it if it won't start.

Northern California

## TOURING AREA: The Northwest

The mountains to the north: the Salmon, the Siskiou and the Trinity Alps are steep and densely timbered. The ski terrain is usually near the 5000′ level. The best nordic skiing is along logging roads or high open ridges. Skiers in the north use lots of klister. They also ski in uncrowded meadows and beautiful forests. Sometimes there is enough snow to ski the coastal Redwood groves. The Trinity Alps and Marble Mountains offer good ski mountaineering. However, the approaches to skiable snow tend to be long.

The Arcata Transit Authority (707) 822-2204 located in Arcata provides lessons, rentals and up-to-date information on snow conditions. One of the most popular ski touring areas in the northwest is Horse Mountain, located 50 miles from Eureka. Skiing along the Horse Mountain Ridge is often excellent. When good skiing conditions exist, there are many comfortable lodges and old logging roads in the northern mountains. The Scott Mountains, where Highway 3 crosses them, are especially good skiing.

Few people have skied Bigfoot country; the region between the Smith River and Happy Camp. The wet snow, steep forested hillsides and damp misty climate discourage most nordic skiers.

## TOURING AREA: Mount Shasta and Mount Lassen

The snow covered slopes of Mount Lassen receive more snow each winter than any other spot in California. The Lassen-Shasta areas are geologically in the Cascades but the wildlife and forests are more typical of the Northern Sierra.

The Fifth Season (916) 926-2776 is located on the right side of North Shasta Road on the way up to the Everitt Memorial Highway. The shop provides rentals, lessons and trail information. In addition to the tours described there is a trail connecting Bunny Flat with Sand Flat. There are several long nordic trails which start at the flats. The trails are marked with orange trapazoid-shaped markers. At times, the trails are machine packed. There are miles of good ski terrain to the northwest of Sand Flat. There is also a distinct possibility that the virgin stands of Shasta Red Fir in this area will be logged.

Castle Lake, a 5 mile drive to the west of Shasta City, is a good alternate ski touring objective on a day when the mountain is stormed in. Take the W.A. Barr road to Castle Lake Road. The lake is at the end of the road.

Mount Lassen Volcanic National Park (916) 595-4444 is a popular ski touring area. There are no services available in the north of the Park in winter. Overnight campers must contact the Park Service for permits and information. The Park Service has a self-register in the Manzanita Meadows parking lot. Manzanita is never crowded and the devastated area is worth seeing. In one sense, it is the site of the biggest avalanche in recent California history. The avalanche was triggered by the volcanic eruption on May 19, 1915. The avalanche of mud, ash and snow completely removed a forest and top soil from the mountain side.

The Lassen Ski Touring Center (916) 595-3376 is located in the Park at the small downhill ski resort. Take Highway 89 north past the Park's south gateway until you come to the resort at the end of the road. Childs Meadow Resort (916) 595-4411 is 10 miles south of the Park on Highway 89/36. Lessons, rentals and maintained ski trails are available at the Meadows.

You have the choice of several tours to volcanic areas in the Park. Beginners can ski to the Sulphur Works where they can see boiling mud pots and the fumaroles. The tour to Bumpass Hell, the most volcanically active area in the Park, is for advanced skiers. At times, the hot springs and warmed creeks will undermine the snow and skiers must watch for weak snow bridges. Emerald and Helen Lakes, five miles up the snow-covered road from the ski resort, are excellent tour destinations for novice skiers. Several active avalanche paths cross the road; the route could be dangerous if an avalanche hazard exists. Ski mountaineers will often ski the southeast bowl of Lassen, the same bowl the summer trail goes up.

The tour up Mount Brokeoff is popular with advanced skiers. Climb the prominent gully above the parking lot ¼ mile before the resort. Follow the drainage to Forest Lake. Then climb the slope south of the lake; from the first ridge you will see the mountain.

Unfortunately the tour to McGowan Lake is popular with snowmobilers as well as skiers. However, it is a lovely area; visit it during the week or some other quiet time. From the intersection of Highway 89 and 39 go north on 89. In 1½ miles you will come to a snow-covered road with the trailhead on the left. Ski along the road for two miles and at the base of a long hill turn to the right. The lake is ¾ mile away.

The trailhead to Wilson Lake is along Highway 89 1 mile south of Childs Meadow. There should be a sign by the snow-covered road. It is a pleasant tour to the lake. Beyond the lake there is good exploring; from some of the ridges there is a fine view of Mount Lassen.

# TOUR 1

**To Shasta Alpine Lodge (7900′ 2408 m)**
**From Everitt Memorial Highway (6700′ 2042 m)**
**Mileage: 5 miles 8 km, round trip**
**Elevation Gain: 1200′ 366 m**
**Classification: Intermediate nordic**
**Season: Late November to early June**
**Topo Map:** *Shasta*

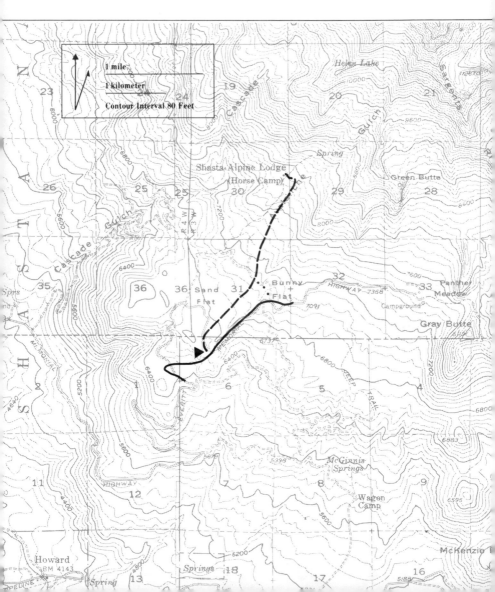

## Features

This tour up to the Shasta Alpine Lodge, at the base of Mt. Shasta, has long been popular. The snow is usually good. Shasta's rocky ridges and snowfields, towering to the northeast, dominate the tour throughout. Storms seem to be speared by Shasta's summit. Lenticular clouds, formed by moist air being lifted above the mountain, are commonly seen. The weather can change rapidly; watch the clouds for approaching storms.

The Sierra Club built the Shasta Alpine Lodge in 1922. The hut is operated on a first-come, first-served basis. The hut is cold and firewood is scare. If you plan to stay overnight, it is often more pleasant to camp outside, retreating to the hut only if necessary.

Novice skiers who don't want to climb to the hut can ski to the gentle terrain around Sand Flat.

## Description

Turn off Interstate 5 at Mt. Shasta City. You can check out at the police station in town. Drive up Everitt Memorial Highway 9 miles to the Sand Flat turnoff. (There is a new section of this highway not shown on the topo map.) A parking area is usually plowed beside the road.

Ski along the snowed-in Sand Flat road for about ¼ mile, until you round the steep ridge to the right. The timber thins after a few hundred yards, and the rest of the tour is through small meadows and open timber. After 1 mile veer north. You can also ski to this point from Bunny Flat, which is ½ mile over the rounded ridge to the right. The parking area for Bunny Flat is 1 mile up the road from the Sand Flat turnoff.

Your destination is the base of Avalanche Gulch, the big bowl on Mt. Shasta. Keep to the northeast, following a wide swale. During the last mile you will pass trees that have been limbed or topped by avalanches. Just before reaching timberline, climb up the bank to the left (north) and ski to the lodge, which is on the edge of timber about 100 yards from the swale.

# TOUR 2

**To Mt. Shasta Summit (14,162′ 4317 m)**
**From Shasta Alpine Lodge (7900′ 2408 m)**
**Mileage: 8 miles 13 km, round trip**
**Elevation Gain: 6300′ 1920 m**
**Classification: Difficult alpine**
**Season: Late April to late June**
**Topo Map:** *Shasta*

## Features

The descent from the summit of Mt. Shasta is a challenge. When the snow is good, it is one of the best ski runs in California. Because this tour takes you across such a range of elevations, you may encounter every conceivable type of snow. The slopes of Shasta are steep and long. If the snow is hard, don't risk a fall. You will need an ice axe and crampons. You may be caught in a white-out at any time, so take your bearings frequently. Skiers have accidentally descended the wrong side of the mountain.

## Description

To reach the lodge at the base of Avalanche Gulch, follow Tour 1. From the lodge climb 1 ¾ miles directly up the steep gulch to the small bench at Helen Lake. Avalanches have swept the entire bench at one time or another, and there are no safe campsites here when an avalanche hazard exists. From the lake climb 800′ north-northeast, and then climb the very steep slope below the Red Banks. Pass the Red Banks on their south end, next to Thumb Rock, and follow the ridge north-northwest to a saddle. From the saddle climb, again north-northeast, to well-named Misery Hill, and then to the summit.

At any point on the way up, if the snow looks too hard to ski on, turn back or leave your skis. Often you cannot ski above the Red Banks, and sometimes not even on the steep slopes below them.

## TOURING AREA: Donner Summit

Donner Summit has been visited by ski tourers since the Gold Rush. Snowshoe Thompson skied over it many times; there is a statue of Snowshoe at the Western America Skisport Museum near Boreal Ridge on Highway 80. The museum is full of old skis and ski mementos. It is a good place to spend a stormy afternoon. The Donner Memorial Park Museum is located along the east shore of Donner Lake. Near the museum is a statue of a pioneer family gazing to the west over Donner Summit. The statue is on a pedestal twenty-two feet high—the depth of snow in 1846, the year the Donner Party was trapped by early storms and forced to winter over. There is a short 2½ mile loop tour at the Park. The State Park system has a very active winter program both in Donner Park and Lake Tahoe. To find out more about it ask at one of the parks or write Sierra Area State Parks, P.O. Drawer D, Tahoma, California 95733, or phone (916) 525-7232.

Donner Summit has been a popular touring area since the transcontinental railroad was built in the winter of 1866-1867. The railroad workers preferred the four inch wide, nine foot long Norwegian "snowshoes" to the webbed Canadian types. According to railroad sources, during that winter "falling wreathes of snow" off Mary Donner Summit, swept fifteen or twenty laborers to their deaths. This was the worst avalanche disaster in California's history.

The only area where skiing is older is at LaPorte where the Forty-Niners used to have downhill races. Sugar Bowl was one of the first ski resorts in the country. The ski tour from Sugar Bowl to Squaw Valley is the start of what was once called the Sierra Skiway, a trail and series of huts from Donner Summit to Yosemite. In the 40's and 50's the Sierra Club built the first three huts but the skiway never reached Echo Summit. The Sierra Club's Clair Tappaan Lodge, located at Norden, is a charming old lodge built in the 1920's. Be careful about parking in the Donner Summit area. This area is crowded and there are new parking laws every year. Traffic fines are very stiff.

Royal Gorge, located at Soda Springs on old Highway 40, provides complete ski touring facilities. There are one hundred miles of machine-packed tracks, rentals, lessons, a nordic ski patrol and a lodge featuring French cooking. A fee is charged for skiing in the tracks. Trail maps and brochures are available. Contact: Royal Gorge Nordic, (916) 426-3871. Lessons and rentals are also available at Clair Tappaan Lodge (916) 426-3632. Donner Ski Ranch and Boreal Ridge have nordic lessons and rentals. Quiet Mountain is a nordic school located in Nevada City (916) 265-9186. They tour near Highways 80, 49, and 20.

In addition to the tours described there are many other places to ski in the Donner area. When the road is covered with snow the tour from the summit down old Highway 40 is fun. You may either shuttle or ski back. The winding ridges north of Castle Pass are fun to explore.

# TOUR 3

To Round Valley (7800′ 2377 m)
From Boreal Ridge (7200′ 2194 m)
Mileage: 5 miles 8 km, round trip
Elevation Gain: 1000′ 305 m
Classification: Novice-to-intermediate nordic
Season: Late December through May
Topo Map: *Donner Pass*

## Features

This trail will often be crowded; a skier should expect to meet snowshoers, snowmobilers and other ski tourers. This tour has been affected by modern technology: before Interstate Highway 80 was built, the tour was 2 miles longer, starting at Norden. Now you may begin the tour from the parking lot at the Boreal Ridge ski area. The tour is also one of the few where you must cross under a freeway overpass.

## Description

Overnight campers will have to leave from Norden, or from the trailhead at the north end of the Boreal Ridge overpass. Overnight parking is not allowed in the Boreal Ridge parking lot. The ski trail begins behind the Sierra Club's Clair Tappaan Lodge at Norden where you may check out plus check for reservations if you want to stay at Peter Grubb hut in Round Valley. Reservations for the hut must be made in advance.

From behind the lodge, climb a moderate draw to the north and turn northwest, skiing on a gently sloping trail. Most likely the route will have been well packed by skiers climbing to the rope tow on Signal Hill. When the trail turns east and begins to climb a moderate slope to the tow, keep on a northwest course. Cross an open meadow and then sidehill north up to the saddle on the ridge. Ski down the packed slope of the ski area to Interstate 80.

If you leave from Boreal Ridge Ski Resort (where you may check out with the ski patrol), cross under the overpass and ski northwest until you come to the edge of the meadow in Castle Valley. Keep to the northwest and climb along the east base of Andesite Ridge to Castle Pass. At the pass, traverse north, contouring around Castle Peak's west ridge. Round Valley is below the ridge between Castle and Basin peaks.

The cabin in Round Valley is Peter Grubb Hut, built by the Sierra Club in the late Thirties. Chapters of the club make reservations for its use well ahead of time. There is a first-aid cache at the hut. If you're camping overnight, ski beyond the hut and find a secluded site in the timber along Castle Creek.

# TOUR 4

To Paradise Valley (7600′ 2316 m)
From Boreal Ridge (7200′ 2195 m)
Mileage: 12 miles 19 km, loop trip
Elevation Gain: 2400′ 732 m
Season: Early January through April
Classification: Difficult nordic
Topo Map: *Donner Pass*

## Features

This tour crosses several passes and avalanche areas, so if the weather has been warm or if it has stormed recently, pick another tour. If done in one day, this tour is a good test of skiing ability. The first few miles follow the busy Round Valley route, but you soon leave the snowshoers and snowmobilers behind. Sheltered, secluded Paradise Valley is an excellent place to camp.

## Description

Follow the description of Tour 3 to Round Valley. From Round Valley ski north through timber to Paradise Valley. Don't climb too high; there is a steep ridge above Paradise Valley, and you might have to head west to get around it and down into the valley. Ski up Paradise Valley to the pass between Paradise and Warren lakes. Snow campers will enjoy an overnight stay in Paradise Valley.

From the pass, sidehill south toward Devils Oven. Be alert for avalanches. Pass Devils Oven on its lower side and climb the moderate slope that begins ¼ mile beyond. Climb the slope until you can traverse along the base of the ridge between Castle and Basin peaks. Don't lose too much elevation, but stay below timberline and be careful crossing any avalanche path. Keep traversing until you are at the foot of Castle Peak. Then ski down across the head of Coon Canyon. Climb around the ridge east of the canyon, and follow a moderate slope up to the top of the east buttress of Castle Peak. Ski southwest until the slope steepens; then work your way down to Boreal Ridge.

Tahoe Region

Photo: Royal Gorge

## TOURING AREA: North Tahoe

There is no other area in California which offers so much nordic skiing or that has so many ski touring centers and events. Most of the centers have rentals, give lessons, maintain trail systems and some have groomed trail systems. The Forest Service has winter programs and they also provide a snow condition — avalanche warning phone (916) 587-2158.

Following is a list of nordic centers in the North Tahoe area:

* Big Chief Guides (916) 587-9813. Located along the Truckee River, just north of Squaw Valley turn-off on Highway 89, it is the oldest nordic school in the area.

* Alpine Meadows (916) 583-4232. This nordic school is located at the Alpine Meadows Lodge.

* Incline Cross Country Ski Area (702) 831-5190, located off Highway 27 in Incline Village on the Executive Golf Course.

* Northstar Nordic Center (916) 562-1010 is on Highway 267 halfway between Truckee and Kings Beach. The snow in Northstar is often colder than in nearby Tahoe. The area is less crowded there and the side roads and trails off the highway are fun to explore.

* Squaw Valley U.S.A. Nordic Center (916) 583-8951 is located in Squaw Valley. Many racers train at the Squaw Olympic Training Center. Jack Kappas, nordic co-director of the center is a Far West Coach for the Junior Olympic team. Most of the skiing is on machine-set tracks in the meadow.

* The Tahoe Nordic Ski Center (916) 583-9858 is located east of Tahoe City. Go east on Highway 28 for 2½ miles and at the Shell Station, turn left on Fabian, right on Village, right on Cedarwood and then left on Country Club. The center sponsors two very popular races: The Great Ski Race is 30 km between the ski center and Truckee and the Triathlon which is ⅓ skiing, ⅓ bicycling, and ⅓ kayaking.

* The Tahoe Donner Ski Touring Center (916) 587-9821 is located in Truckee. Take the Donner Park exit on Highway 80 and head east toward Truckee. Turn left on Northwoods Blvd. The Far West Ski Association and the center co-sponsor an annual Donner Trail ski tour. In addition to the center there are many fine places to ski. Almost every canyon along the west shore of Lake Tahoe has snow-covered roads. The Brockway Summit area has many good tours.

The tour into Five Lakes Basin where the Sierra Club maintains Bradley Hut is a popular tour. The tour begins 1½ miles below the Alpine Meadows ski area. From the road climb up below the avalanche paths on the west side and then follow a steep gully to the basin.

Paige Meadows is popular with beginning nordic skiers. Go
south from Tahoe City on Highway 89 about 1½ miles. Turn
right on Pine then right on Tahoe Park Heights Drive. Take
the middle fork and then turn left on Silver Tip Street. Signs
may be obscured. There is a series of meadows separated by
islands of aspen, pine and fir. Nordic skiers enjoy skiing up the
first few miles of Blackwood Canyon. The State Park System
has marked ski trails up General Creek at Sugar Pine Point.
There is a year-round campground with a checkout station
where there should be trail maps available.

The long day tour to Highway 89 from the Rest Stop before
Donner Pass is most enjoyable. Ski to the northeast down Euer
Valley to Carpenter Valley and Highway 89. Skiing the open
fields and hillsides through the Truckee Burn and down
through quiet Carpenter and Independence Valleys is fun for
intermediate skiers. The University of California at Berkeley
has a research station along Sagehen Creek; it is best not to
bother it. Make sure you park your car off Highway 89 or you
could get a ticket.


# TOUR 5

To Squaw Valley (6300′ 1920 m)
From Sugar Bowl (7000′ 2134 m)
Mileage: 13 miles 21 km, shuttle tour
Elevation Gain: 3000′ 914 m
Classification: Intermediate alpine or intermediate-to-
   difficult nordic
Season: Early February to early May
Topo Maps: *Donner Pass, Granite Chief, Tahoe*

## Features
This is a classic North Tahoe tour. Skiers made this tour long
before there were any developed ski areas at Squaw Valley or
even Sugar Bowl—and Sugar Bowl is one of the oldest ski
resorts in California.

This is a fair weather tour. It crosses a few avalanche paths,
and a third of it follows high, windswept ridges. Intermediate
skiers should plan on taking two days. Since the tour includes
some steep downhill sections, intermediate nordic skiers
shouldn't attempt it when the snow is icy or when there is a
breakable crust.

# Description

Park at Norden or in the Sugar Bowl garage. Whoever is going to pick you up at Squaw Valley can notify the authorities if you do not show up on time. If you do not ride the lift, get an early morning start so as not to get in the way of the alpine skiers.

Cross the railroad tracks and follow the lift that leads into Sugar Bowl. Pass the main lodge and ski up below the Lincoln chair lift until you are on the edge of the cirque just under the top of the lift. You can avoid the first 3 miles — and 1300′ — by taking the chair lift to the top of Mt. Lincoln. The resort will sell a single-ride ticket. Turn left and follow the ski run's gentle-to-moderate slopes to the top of Mt. Lincoln. As you near the top, resist the temptation to traverse across the east bowl of Lincoln to the Lincoln-Anderson ridge. In the early Sixties, a tourer was killed in an avalanche from the east bowl. Before you head southeast down the ridge toward Anderson Peak, you should be able to see the block house on Mt. Lincoln's summit.

It often seems as though the ridge to Anderson Peak is one of the windiest places in the Sierra. There is always a big cornice on the ridge's east face, so if a storm comes up be careful to stay away from this area. Sometimes there are markers in the snow along the ridge to help skiers keep their bearings. There might be a rescue sled cached along the ridge. Most of the route was once marked with yellow triangles, some of which remain. Each one showed the compass bearing and distance to the next triangle. Where the ridge begins to be timbered, veer right and climb at a gentle angle toward the base of Anderson Peak.

The Sierra Club's Benson Hut is located in the timber on Anderson's north ridge. The hut is usually reserved far ahead by members of the club, but it may be available to others. If you are interested in using it, ask at the club's Clair Tappaan Lodge in Norden. The Sierra Club has had a difficult time keeping its huts in shape. The way visitors treat them will determine how they will be managed in the future. If you stop in a hut, leave it in better condition than you found it.

To get around Anderson Peak, climb to the right (southwest) and cut around the west half of the peak to the next ridge, which leads to Tinker (or Tinker's) Knob. On a clear day you can see Mt. Diablo far in the southwest. Continue southeast along the ridge, skiing to the left of Tinker Knob. Beyond the knob, ski down the steep slope for 500′ and then traverse south. Don't ski too low; the route heads south-southeast toward the gap above Mountain Meadow Lake. Follow a bench, and after 1 mile come into a shallow valley leading to a small lake. Ski up the valley to a saddle. From here you can look down Shirley Canyon (not named on the topo map) and see the orange Blythe Ice Arena, built for the 1960 Winter Olympics.

There are two routes down to Squaw Valley. You can work directly down Shirley Canyon, or you can ski to the base of the Shirley Lake chair lift, climb the ski run under the lift, and ski down one of the main runs to Squaw Valley Lodge. If you ski down Shirley Canyon, avoid the avalanche paths south of the creek.

Photo: Andy Schilpp

# TOUR 6

To the Headwaters of Incline Creek (9200′ 2804 m)
From the Mt. Rose Highway (8900′ 2713 m)
Mileage: 5 miles 8 km, round trip
Elevation Gain: 300′ 91 m
Classification: Novice nordic
Season: First snow, often the last two weeks of November
Topo Map: *Mt. Rose* (Nevada)

# Features

This is one of several novice tours along the Mt. Rose highway. For years skiers impatient for the touring season to begin have skied the "Mt. Rose sand dunes" when there was not enough snow anywhere else. The combination of high altitude and sparse ground cover makes it possible to ski on a few inches of snow. The meadows and rounded hillsides are covered with decomposed granite, which provides a smooth surface.

The views are good. Lake Tahoe and the peaks on the rim of the basin on the west are visible on a clear day. There are also occasional glimpses to the east of the Great Basin Ranges in Nevada.

In early winter the Mt. Rose area is cold and windy; take plenty of clothing. There are no avalanche paths near Tahoe Meadows, south of the highway, but once a few feet of snow have fallen, most of the steep slopes around the meadows should be considered dangerous. There have been several avalanche accidents in this region.

Washoe pine, which most botanists believe to be a hybrid of Jeffrey pine and ponderosa pine, can be found around the Galena Creek campground. This curious tree looks nothing at all like either Jeffrey or ponderosa.

# Description

Just west of the summit of the Mt. Rose highway is a building. A road starts just below this building and climbs gradually west, passing an occasional whitebark pine. One of the delights of this part of the tour is the view: the interior ranges south of Virginia City, parts of the Sierra far to the south toward Yosemite, Slide Mountain right across the canyon, Stevens Peak in the Carson Range at the headwaters of the Truckee River, Pyramid Peak and Mt. Tallac with Desolation Valley between them, Rubicon Peak with its rocky summit knoll — all are clearly visible. Clear days are not as common here as they once were, but when one does occur you can spend hours absorbing the scenery and identifying landmarks.

Continue up the road, rounding a bend and entering the canyon above Incline Lake. The road levels off a bit as it continues through lodgepole forest. The leveled terraces on the ridge north of the Mt. Rose relay station are part of a Forest Service erosion-control project. After about ¾ mile the tour reaches its highest point at a broad saddle covered with whitebark and lodgepole pines. From here we can look east across steep terrain to the summit of Mt. Rose. From the saddle, the road climbs up to the microwave relay station, crossing some dangerous avalanche paths. American Telephone and Telegraph Company built the tram, with its green buildings, so that its service personnel would not have to travel along the dangerous road during the winter.

In the canyon below are several small, sheltered meadows. If there is enough snow, intermediate skiers can ski down the creek toward Incline Lake and then return to the start of the tour by skiing up Tahoe Meadows.

## TOURING AREA: South Tahoe

This is Snowshoe Thompson country. He roamed over the hills and meadows for twenty years carrying the mail when the Pony Express floundered in the deep Sierra snow. Few modern skiers could equal his regular schedule by carrying a sixty pound pack from Carson Valley to Placerville in two days.

Telemark Country Sports (916) 577-6811 is located at Yanks Station near Meyers on Highway 50. The center maintains machine tracks on the Tahoe Paradise golf course. The center also offers tours to Hope Valley, Luther Pass and the Echo Summit area. Echo Nordic Center (916) 659-7154 is located in the Echo Summit ski area and offers rentals, lessons, trail maps and maintained trails.

Novices who wish to ski in Thompson's tracks can ski along broad, level Hope Valley if they don't mind dodging snow-mobiles. Grass Meadow on Luther Pass provides a more relaxed touring environment. There are some very long novice tours along the Carson River. Try the one from Hope Valley to Charity Valley by way of Faith Valley. You can also tour along the road that goes south from Hope Valley and contours up around the base of Pickett Peak. After a long, gradual climb to Burnside Lake, ski down the steep slope beside Hot Springs Creek. Plan to wait for your ride back by soaking in Grovers Hot Springs. Take a swim suit, a towel and a dollar to pay the entrance fee.

Around Lake Tahoe the best nordic touring is in the Jeffrey-ponderosa-lodgepole forests near Fallen Leaf Lake. During winter and early spring the Forest Service conducts natural history tours at several locations. Ask at the ranger station in South Tahoe.

The Kirkwood Ski Touring Center (209) 258-8864 is located next to the Kirkwood Inn on Highway 88. The Inn is a log building formerly used as a Pony Express station. Glen Jobe is the director of the center and is a U.S. Olympic Biathlon skier. The center maintains a racing track and holds one of the most challenging races in the Sierra. The 12 mile long race from Echo Summit to Kirkwood is held near the end of March. Kirkwood Meadow is an ideal place for beginning nordic skiers.

Carson Pass is ideal for nordic touring. Highway 88 is above 7,000′ for almost twenty miles. The tour south from Carson Pass toward Elephants Back and Round Top will let advanced skiers test their telemark skills; the area always has good snow. Take care when skiing near any of the reservoirs; the ice may be unsafe because of water release. Be sure to stop at the Carson Pass turn-out and see the granite monument to Snowshoe Thompson.

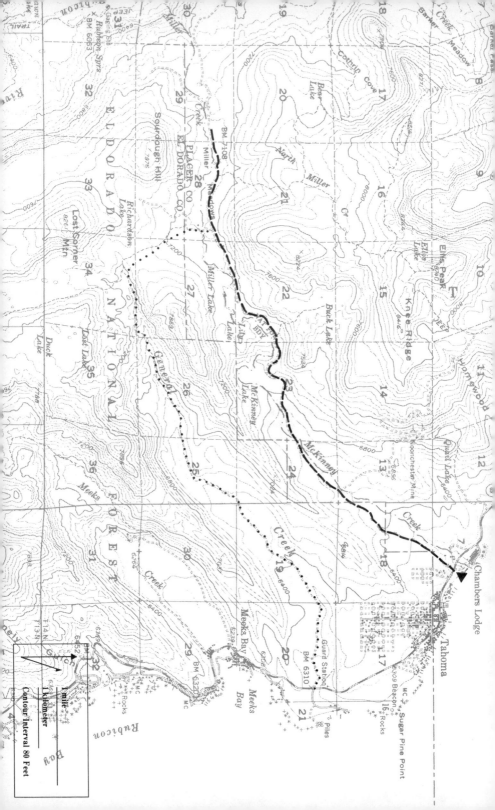

# TOUR 7

To Miller Meadows (7100' 2164 m) along the
  McKinney Creek Road
From Highway 89 (6300' 1920 m)
Mileage: 10 miles 16 km, round trip
Elevation Gain: 800' 244m
Classification: Novice nordic
Season: Late December through April
Topo Map: *Tahoe*

## Features

This is a long, gentle tour through red fir and lodgepole pine
forest. It also passes some magnificent cedars that escaped log-
gers back in mining and railroad days. These large cedars,
their bark covered with staghorn lichen, grow in isolated
islands in the chaparral. Most of the tour is through timber,
and without map and compass you can easily lose the road. If
you lose it, turn east and eventually you will reach Highway
89.

Some of the cross country events for the 1960 Olympics were
held along the flats beside McKinney Creek. Since the Olympics, most of the land has been subdivided (McKinney Estates),
but a wandering skier may still come across an old cleared ski
trail.

## Description

South of Chambers at Homewood, on Tahoe's west shore,
Highway 89 crosses McKinney Creek. The McKinney Road
turns off the highway 200 yards south of the crossing. Follow
the road southwest through dense timber. When you cross
McKinney Creek, be careful if you are crossing on a snow
bridge. If the bridge isn't hard enough that a ski-pole handle is
difficult to push through, it may collapse under your weight.
The road climbs above McKinney Lake and skirts the north
shores of McKinney, Lily and Miller lakes. Miller Meadows is
¼ mile west of Miller Lake.

For those who don't want to return the way they came, there is
an intermediate nordic tour back to the road. Ski southeast
from Miller Meadows for 1 mile; then turn northeast and ski
down General Creek to Highway 89.

# TOUR 8

To Desolation Valley (8100′ 2469 m)
From Echo Summit (7400′ 2256 m)
Mileage: 14 miles 23 km, round trip
Elevation Gain: 1100′ 335 m
Classification: Intermediate nordic
Season: Early January through mid-May
Topo Map: *Fallen Leaf Lake*
Wilderness permit: Obtain at Placerville or South Shore

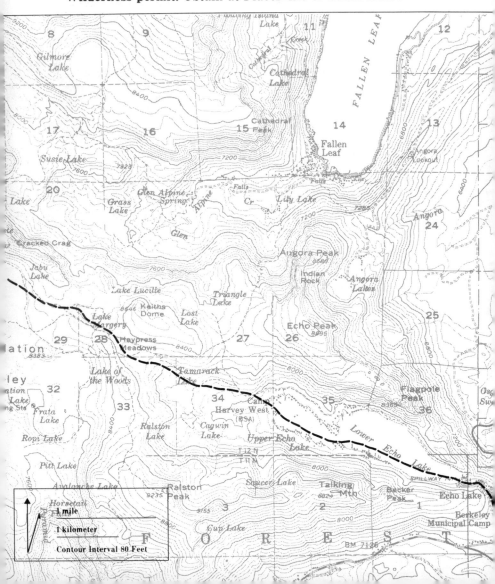

# Features

The tour into Desolation Valley, a large, glacially scoured basin, is the most popular tour in the South Tahoe region. On a weekend in February or March you will probably meet other touring parties every few miles. Once you reach the rolling, open terrain of Desolation Valley, however, you should be able to find a secluded campsite. If not, find one below Lake Aloha in the timber. Novices can ski as far as Tamarack Lake if the snow is good, but if the snow surface is wet, they should ski out before evening shadows make a breakable crust. If you plan a shuttle tour to Twin Bridges, ski down the steep draw ½ mile west of Horsetail Falls. Other interesting shuttle tours through Desolation Valley include (1) touring down Alpine Creek to Fallen Leaf Lake (a 2000′ drop), and (2) skiing over Mosquito Pass to Squaw Valley or even Donner Summit.

# Description

On Highway 50 about one mile west of Echo Summit, turn north onto a narrow paved road marked by the Berkeley Camp sign. Drive up the road almost ½ mile, to where a road to the left (the road to Echo Lake) has been cleared for about 100 feet. The tour begins on the snow-covered road.

The first mile of the route has usually been packed by snowmobiles and hikers. After a few hundred feet, the road curves to the right (north) and then climbs northwest around the east shoulder of Becker Peak. For a short distance you can look down on the Upper Truckee valley and Lake Tahoe. The view is great at night when the lights below are sparkling in the cold air.

Continue on the road, skiing through the forest of lodgepole pine, ponderosa pine and red fir. From the crest of the small hill above Lower Echo Lake, ski down the road and out onto the lake. In the spring be sure the lake is still frozen. If in doubt, ski along the southwest shore. Often the wind will sweep away snow, exposing bare ice. If the wind is blowing hard enough and in the right direction, a sail such as a tent's rain fly held between yourself and a companion provides an elegant way to cross the lake.

Once across Lower Echo Lake, climb up the left side of the inlet and ski through a grove of lodgepoles onto Upper Echo Lake. Leave Upper Echo Lake at the right of its inlet, and after a short flat section, climb some bumpy terrain. Stay well away from the creek, because there are a series of small gullies next to the creek which are awkward to cross. Beyond the gullies, climb northwest through open juniper woodland. Keep

well to the right of the creek, climbing up the rounded, rolling terrain. Climb to the right on the wide, sloping bench north of Tamarack Lake, and then sidehill 200′ up a steep open slope at the top of the bench. This slope might slide during periods of avalanche hazard.

When you get to the lodgepole-hemlock forest, veer more northwest. After a short climb up a moderate slope you will come to Haypress Meadows, which have a small, corniced ridge above their west side. Ski up the meadows. From the upper end of the meadows, Dicks and Jacks peaks can be seen, framed by timber. Veer left and ski down the moderate, rolling slope, keeping the corniced ridge in sight to the west. Some of the small slopes below the ridge could avalanche, so don't ski too close to the ridge.

Ski down the bumps to Lake Margery. This lake, with its densely timbered shore, is exceptionally pretty after a snow-fall. Leaving this lake, climb northwest through a lodgepole forest 1 mile, to Desolation Valley. The rocky hump to the right lies between Desolation Valley and Fallen Leaf Lake. A short climb to its top will reward you with a view of Pyramid Peak and the Crystal Range to the west, and the back of Mount Tallac to the north. Lake Aloha can be reached by skiing north-west down the slope.

# TOUR 9

To Mt. Tallac Summit (9735′ 2967 m)
From Highway 89 (6300′ 1920 m)
Mileage: 8 miles 13 km, round trip
Elevation Gain: 3435′ 1047 m
Classification: Intermediate alpine
Season: Mid-March to late April
Topo Map: *Fallen Leaf Lake*

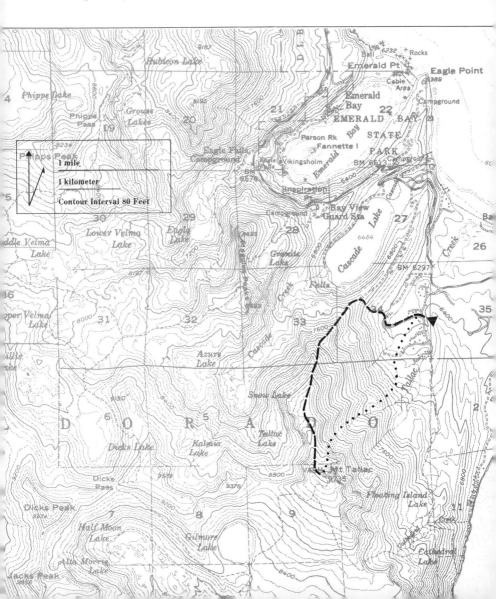

## Features

A yearly spring ascent of Mt. Tallac is a tradition among ski tourers in the Tahoe basin. The run down from the summit is one of the best around Lake Tahoe.

Start up Tallac early in the morning; the sun lights up Tahoe in a special way. An early start allows time for a leisurely lunch before the sun softens the snow too much for a pleasant run down.

## Description

Park along Highway 89 near Tallac Creek or, if the lateral road is plowed, as close as possible to the base of Mt. Tallac's north ridge. Climb to the base of the north ridge and work your way up this steep, rounded ridge. The crest will become more obvious as you climb. The view from the top, one of the best in the Tahoe basin, includes the Crystal Range beyond Desolation Valley in the west, and the peaks north and south of Lake Tahoe.

There are several runs down. You can ski down the ascent route or down one of the bowls north of the summit. Don't go on this tour if there is an avalanche hazard. Several of the upper bowls avalanche regularly, as the absence of timber testifies.

For a steeper, more direct route up Mt. Tallac from the starting point, climb up the bowl northeast of the summit.

# TOUR 10

To Meiss Lake (8300′ 2530 m)
From Carson Pass (8600′ 2621 m)
Mileage: 7 miles 11 km, round trip
Elevation gain: 700′ 213 m
Classification: Intermediate nordic
Season: Early December through May
Topo maps: *Markleeville, Silver Lake*

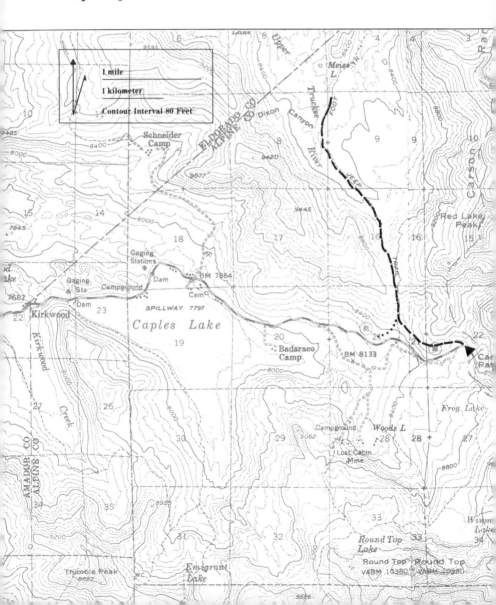

## Features

Confident novices will enjoy this tour, although they may have  to do a little traversing and kick turning on the steeper slopes. This tour is the first 3½ miles of an 11-mile intermediate nordic tour to Echo Summit. Intermediate skiers can also tour 5 more miles down the Truckee River to Highway 89.

## Description

Park on Highway 88 at the turnout at Carson Pass. From the pass, work your way west, sidehilling at a slight upward angle for ½ mile and then leveling off. As you curve around the hillside, you pass several species of conifers: a few very large specimens of western white pine, also called silver pine, some lodgepole pine, some red fir, and an occasional wind-beaten juniper. If the snow isn't too deep, you will probably become aware of the buried aspen trees when you catch your ski tips on them.

If you climb too high, you will have to traverse some steep avalanche paths below the southwest ridge of Red Lake Peak. It is better to drop down to the edge of the forest. You will come out in a timbered bowl below the avalanche paths. To the northwest is an obvious rounded saddle. The climb up to it is the steepest part of the tour. Stay out of the gullies; switchback up the slope between them. It is poor route finding practice to ski unnecessarily in an avalanche path.

From the saddle, Round Top Peak dominates the view to the south. Elephants Back, with its steep, glaciated northeast face, is visible in the southeast. Ski north, staying well to the right of the gully. Lake Tahoe and the peaks on the eastern rim of Rockbound Valley come into view as you ski down from the saddle. Notice the large cornice on the ridge to the west; avalanches from the cornice and the pillow below it keep the slope bare of timber. Continue down the moderate slope to the meadow visible in the northwest. Stay well above the east bank of the gully here.

Out in the meadow, cross the Upper Truckee River. During warm weather beware of collapsing snow bridges. The meadow, fringed by lodgepoles, was made for nordic skiers. The two cabins here are leased by the Forest Service to a cattleman who brings his herds to the meadow for the summer.

Ski along the east bank of the river for 1 mile to where you can see a large meadow in the northeast. Meiss Lake is at the far end of this meadow. The cliffs northeast of Meiss Lake drop off into Round Lake, an easy 1-mile tour from Meiss Lake. It is a moderate-to-difficult 4-mile tour from Round Lake to Highway 89.

East Side of the Sierra

## TOURING AREA: Mammoth

The San Joaquin River canyon acts like a giant funnel channeling storms toward Mammoth. Since the Sierra crest is lower there than to the north and south, storms pile up. The storms are always more intense and the snowpack deeper at Mammoth than in surrounding areas. The elevation and location on the east slope of the Sierra cause colder temperatures which in turn create excellent ski conditions. There is more hard wax skiing in Mammoth than in almost any other place in California. The cold temperatures also prolong avalanche hazards. Most of the Mammoth area is covered by a smooth layer of pumice, a remnant of volcanic activity. The smooth pumice carpet enables one to ski on only a few inches of snow.

The Forest Service (619) 934-2505 maintains a 3 to 6 kilometer ski track in back of the Mammoth Visitor Center located on the north side of Highway 203 just before you reach Mammoth Village. If you plan on skiing into the backcountry, stop there to pick up your wilderness permit and check the avalanche forecast.

Most of the ski shops in Mammoth rent nordic skis. A few of them such as Sports & Trails, Doug Kittredge's and Uphill Sports also have lessons. The Sierra Meadows Ski Touring Center (619) 934-6161 is located on Sherwin Creek road just off Old Mammoth Road. The center provides full services. The Mammoth Cross Country Ski Resort (619) 934-2442, located at Tamarack Lodge on Twin Lakes off the Lake Mary Road also provides complete services. The ski touring in the upper Mammoth Lakes Basin is excellent. The 42 kilometer Mammoth Marathon is held in the basin every February. Sierra Ski Touring (619) 934-4495 specializes in group tours, wilderness ski tours, nordic downhill and avalanche schools. It is directed by David Beck, P.O. Box C-9, Mammoth Lakes, Ca. 93546.

There is vast nordic ski terrain between June Lake and Mammoth. The areas around Glass Creek, Deadman Creek, Dry Creek and Mono Craters have miles of snow-covered rolling terrain. There is fine intermediate and expert touring in upper Glass Creek. Within a few years there should be a marked trail connecting June Lake and Mammoth. Snowmobiles are not as common in the Mammoth area as they once were. However, you will occasionally meet a snowmobile group especially to the east of Highway 395.

During a good snow year the tour into the ghost town of Bodie is unique. Bodie is a State Historic Park, there are two rangers who live there all year long. Bodie is a 26 mile round trip tour from the turn-off 7 miles south of Bridgeport or a 20 mile round trip tour from Highway 167. The days may be warm but the nights near Bodie can be very cold. Bridgeport, to the west on Highway 395, is often the coldest spot in California with temperatures of 20 to 30 degrees colder than Mammoth. Check on snow and road conditions at the county courthouse in Bridgeport.

The Sierra backcountry is accessible from many parts of the Mammoth area. The U.S. Marine Corps has a Mountain Warfare Training Center off the Sonora Pass road to the north of Bridgeport. The Sonora Pass road is often rutted with snowmobile tracks. If there is no avalanche hazard, the Tioga Pass road is a better access to the high country. The more classic ski routes to Tuolumne Meadows are over Mono or Donohue Passes. The best route to Donohue Pass is by way of the high trail from Agnew Meadows and Thousand Island Lake. The route from Agnew Meadows to Shadow Lake is often icy or avalanche prone just before the Shadow Lake area. Many local Mammoth skiers like to ski up to Mammoth Pass in the upper lakes basin. The best early season snow is often found on the first part of the San Joaquin Ridge tour. The tour from Mammoth Pass to Red's Meadow Hot Springs is popular. Be careful, however, it's difficult to find your way down or up the hill above the hot springs. New soft snow makes the climb up very difficult. There are several large slide paths which cross the road from Minaret Summit down to Agnew Meadows.

The Forest Service also sets nordic ski tracks at Rock Creek and the June Lake junction.

# TOUR 11

To Sawtooth Ridge from Twin Lakes (7100' 2164 m)
Camp at (8300' 2530 m)
Climb Matterhorn Peak (12,264' 3738 m)
Mileage: 10 miles 16 km, round trip
Elevation Gain: 4000' 1219 m
Classification: Intermediate-to-difficult alpine
Season: From mid-April through June
Topo map: *Matterhorn Peak*
Wilderness permit: Obtain at Bridgeport Ranger Station

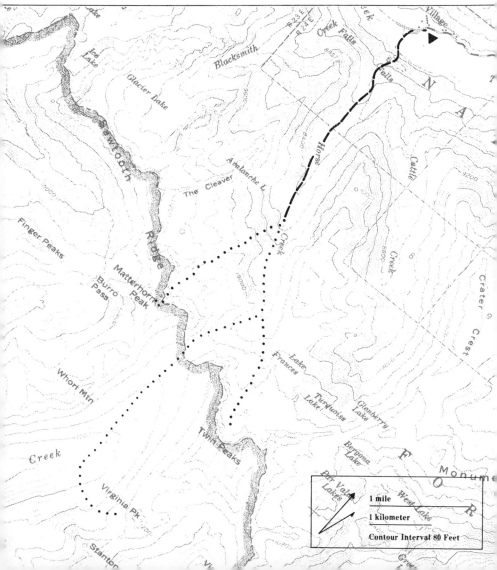

## Features

The touring below compact Sawtooth Ridge has much to offer. The road to Twin Lakes is plowed all winter, assuring access to the starting point of the tour. Ski mountaineers will appreciate the relatively short climb to the base camp on Horse Creek, and the runs on the snowfields and glaciers above the camp. Novice nordic skiers can explore the gentle terrain along Robinson Creek. The tour to Virginia Pass is intermediate to difficult, depending on the snow. From the pass one can tour down to Return Creek and then southeast to Tuolumne Meadows.

## Description

Check out when you get your wilderness permit. The nearest ranger station is on Highway 395 about 5 miles northwest of Bridgeport. In Bridgeport, take the signed road 13 miles west to the head of Twin Lakes.

From the parking area, cross Robinson Creek on the footbridge. Keeping to the south, enter a stand of fir and pine, and cross Horse Creek on a log bridge. The first few miles of the trail may be free of snow during April. If they are, follow the trail as it switchbacks up the hill east of Horse Creek Falls. If not, work your way on skis up the hill.

After 600′ the slope levels off, becoming more gentle near the campsite. Continue up the gentle slope to the last forested flat area (8300′). This is the last sheltered campsite. Be sure not to camp too far up the canyon, where camps are in danger from falling rocks and avalanches. Frost wedging (nivation) causes rockfalls if days are warm, snowmelt water is available and nights are well below freezing. Continuously cold or warm temperatures will not result in the release of rocks. In the Sawtooth region in the spring, it is not unusual to hear the rumble of falling rocks. Rockfall is most common during the first few hours after the sun has begun to warm up a slope, when the ice that has "glued" rock to a cliff is melting. In addition, frost wedging can move rocks over small horizontal distances. The summit of Mt. Whitney and many other nonglaciated high plateaus are nivation plains, where alternate freezing and thawing of meltwater has created jumbles of rock.

Several good ski ascents can be made from this campsite. The easiest is that of Twin Peaks and the most difficult is that of Matterhorn Peak.

Matterhorn Peak: If the snow is icy this is a difficult climb, and it would be wiser to take one of the other side tours instead. Remember that it is colder at higher elevations, so the snow will be harder.

From camp climb the steep 600′ slope along Horse Creek and continue south to the first major tributary on the right. Follow this streamcourse up, passing a small tarn. Soon the east face of Matterhorn Peak becomes obvious above. The route leads left up the east couloir. Be careful—the slope is steep and in the shade and you will need an ice axe. A skier was killed in an avalanche below the east couloir.

Twin Peaks: Climb the steep 600′ ridge above camp, following Horse Creek. The route is very simple. Follow the creek in a more or less straight line southeast to the base of Twin Peaks. This is the highest point you can reach on skis—3 miles from camp and 3000′ above it. Many skiers turn around here, having come for the run down to camp. If you continue, climb 600′ to the col between the two peaks. You will need an ice axe. Once up the col, it is an easy walk to the higher (west) peak.

Virginia Peak: Climb from the campsite along Horse Creek. After the first steep section (600′), the route becomes moderate. At the drainage fork just before the base of Matterhorn Peak's east ridge, turn right (southwest) and head for the pass between Matterhorn Peak and the Twin Peaks ridge. Ski down from the pass 1½ miles to Virginia Peak. If you climb to the summit, you will have to leave your skis about 800′ below the summit.

# TOUR 12

**To San Joaquin Ridge (10,255′ 3,126 m)**
**From Mammoth Mountain Ski Area (9000′ 2743 m)**
**Mileage: 5 miles 8 km, round trip**
**Elevation Gain: 1200′ 366 m**
**Classification: Intermediate nordic**
**Season: Mid-December to mid-May**
**Topo Map:** *Devils Postpile*

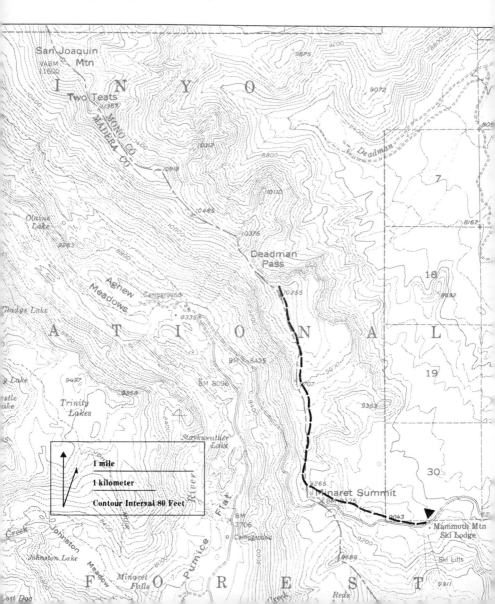

# Features

The climb along the crest from Minaret Summit to peak 10255 is one of the best nordic tours in California. The snow is usually excellent. Often while one skis on windpacked powder, using hard blue wax, tourers below will be trying to ski on cold snow whose surface is wet from the sun. During storms, a southwest wind blows constantly along the crest, causing long windrows of snow to form behind every rock and tree. The windrows form giant ripples on the snow, giving the descending skiers the feeling they are on a roller coaster. If you want a smoother run, or if there is so much snow that the ripples are too steep, you can ski down the lee side of the crest on smooth snow.

One of the nice things about this tour is that you don't have to reach any high point to enjoy the view; it is with you along most of the route. To the west, Banner Peak and Mt. Ritter rise massively above the more delicate Minarets. To the southeast, the White Mountains and Boundary Peak rise out of the desert. The White Mountains have a mysterious air when the sun is setting, as they capture the last golden light when the foothills are dark.

Most of the tour is exposed to wind and sun. Take along warm, windproof clothing and lotion for protection from sunburn. If you see dark clouds rolling up the San Joaquin River canyon, turn back; the crest is a bad place in a white-out.

# Description

Go west from Highway 395 to Mammoth on Highway 203 and turn right on the road that leads to the ski area and Minaret Summit. If the road to Minaret Summit is closed by snow, use the ski resort's parking lot. Parking is very difficult on weekends. If you arrive late in the day, you might have to add about 2 miles of parking lot and road to the tour.

Ski below (north of) the road, paralleling it to Minaret Summit, unless the snow is shallow, when the best route is on the road. Turn north at Minaret Summit, passing through open stands of lodgepole and hemlock. About 100 yards up the crest from the road is a Forest Service vista point. Since this point is slightly to the windward side of the crest, it is often bare of snow. It is a good place to stop, check your wax and enjoy the view. From here, all the Minarets and many other nearby points of interest can be identified.

Continue north along the crest. About ½ mile from the vista point, the ridge narrows, from here the east side is steep and in many places corniced. Be careful; stay about twice as far from the edge as you think necessary. Except on this short stretch

of a few hundred feet, there is always a meadow or a flat to the east which is sheltered from the wind. There is an especially big meadow beyond where the ridge narrows.

As you climb the crest, whitebark pines become the dominant trees. The whitebark pines live in an environment as dry as the interior desert to the east. Most of the snow that falls around the trees is blown away, so in spring there is little meltwater to soak into the soil.

When snow conditions are bad, you can ski in the meadow just beyond the narrow portion of the ridge rather than touring on up the crest. If you continue, keep climbing on the exposed crest until you come to the high point (10,255′) overlooking Deadman Pass. This is the highest point on the tour. To the northwest you can see the top of Mt. Lyell. The view along the crest includes Two Teats, more than 3 miles to the north, and San Joaquin Mountain, just beyond. June Lake is almost due north. The best way to reach June Lake from the Mammoth Mountain ski area is to ski down to Deadman Creek and skirt the base of the east side of White Wing Crest climbing slowly toward the June Mountain ski area.

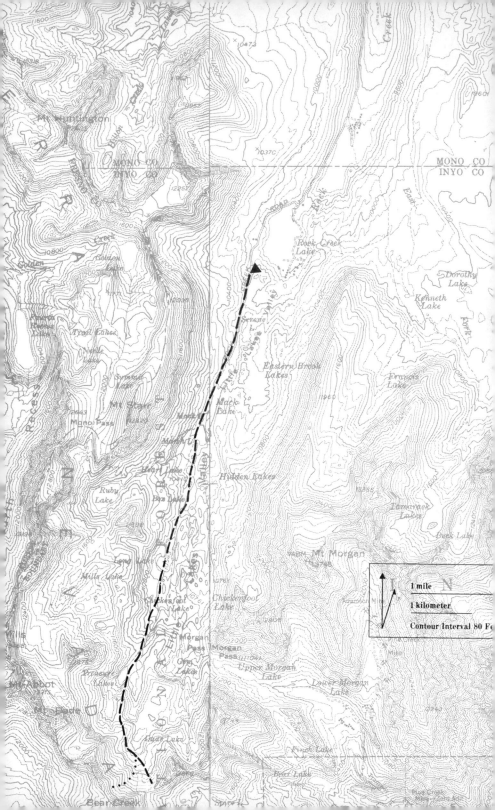

1 mile

N

1 kilometer

Contour Interval 80 Fe

# TOUR 13

Toward Bear Creek Spire (13,713' 4180 m)
From Rock Creek Roadend (10,250' 3124 m)
Mileage: 12 miles 19 km, round trip
Elevation Gain: 2150' 655 m
Classification: Difficult alpine (first 5 miles suitable for
 intermediate nordic skiers)
Season: December through June
Topo Maps: *Mt. Tom, Mt. Abbott*
Wilderness Permit: Obtain in Bishop or Mammoth

## Features

The canyon carved by Rock Creek is long and, unlike most canyons on the east side of the Sierra, fairly gentle. Nordic skiers will enjoy the lower canyon, and when the snow is good they can ski into the higher bowls. The road itself (before it is plowed) is a good tour. For nordic skiers who want to ski on moderate terrain and also see the eastern High Sierra in winter, this tour is ideal. The bowls below Bear Creek Spire are large and open, providing some excellent late-season skiing. Some avalanche paths cross the road, so don't tour into this area when an avalanche hazard exists.

The Rock Creek Winter Lodge is located before Rock Creek Lake. The lodge is very popular among ski tourers. Most winters you have to ski a few miles into the lodge or if you have reservations they will pick you up and bring you in by Snowcat.

## Description

Check out at the Mammoth or Bishop ranger station when you get your wilderness permit. The road up Rock Creek begins at Toms Place, just north of Sherwin Summit on Highway 395. It goes 11 miles up Rock Creek, the last 2 are unpaved. The end of the road (10,250') is not plowed until late spring.

From the roadend, follow a southwestward route, which coincides with the summer trail, 3 miles to Long Lake. Near the Long Lake inlet, leave the trail (if you ever found it) and go in a slightly more westward direction, following the stream 1 mile to Treasure Lakes. Good campsites exist in the last timbered area before Treasure Lakes. Beyond Long Lake the tour is an easy, rolling uphill route, only the last mile to the Treasure Lakes is moderately steep. On spring corn snow it takes between 2½ and 4 hours to reach the campsites from the roadend.

From the campsites climb the moderately steep ridge between the two southernmost Treasure Lakes. Follow the ridge until you can traverse southeast into the large bowls under Bear Creek Spire. The bowls provide ideal skiing. They are sheltered from the wind and the last afternoon sun, but they catch enough early sun to soften the snow surface.

Climbers who want to make the summit of Bear Creek Spire should be prepared for a steep climb. They will need at least an ice axe. Most skiers will find the skiing in the bowls reward enough.

## TOURING AREA: Owens Valley and Death Valley

When the Owens Valley has snow, a nordic skier can wander at will. A tour through the sage and creosote brush on the higher alluvial fans is a unique experience. Perhaps tourers from Mongolia would understand the open grandeur one feels when skiing in the desert. For ski mountaineers the eastern side of the Sierra is unparalled. Climbers cannot resist the steep, short routes to the summits along the main crest. The higher east side can be especially stark; a world of white with only occasional trees to supply contrast to the towering rock walls.

Storms can blow up very rapidly. A skier should always be prepared to retreat immediately or sit out a storm. Avalanche hazards persist for long periods along the high, cold crest of the Sierra. Be very careful when skiing during the first part of winter, before the snow begins to settle in the spring. Another hazardous time to tour near slide paths is the first week of the spring thaw.

Often you will begin a tour skiing in wet slush and arrive at the highest point on cold windslab. Snow conditions vary. High ridges blocking storms, and at times generating storms of their own, can create different snow depths and, different avalanche conditions in adjacent canyons. Unless you tour an area often and are familiar with it, be wary. Strong intermediate nordic skiers with metal-edged skis, stiff-soled boots and good downhill ski technique have recently skied most of the tours described. The nordic descent of Elderberry Canyon, from the summit of Mt. Tom, is one of the most challenging ski descents in the area.

Novice nordic skiers will find some ski touring at the roadhead of Highway 168 above Bishop. The Horseshoe Meadows-- Cottonwood Lakes area has excellent nordic skiing. It's the best way into the Kern Plateau. The road up to Cottonwood

Lakes is often blocked by snow, fallen rocks or a gate. It is not unusual to see cars trapped by storms and left for the winter. Some areas on the eastern Sierra are closed so as not to disturb a small population of Bighorn sheep. For a wilderness permit, snow and road conditions, contact the Forest Service at Lone Pine (619) 876-5542.

Glacer Lodge, above Big Pine, is not open in the winter. The Palisade School of Mountaineering in Bishop (619) 873-5037 offers ski mountaineering and mountain medicine courses.
base. The school offers ski mountaineering and mountain medicine courses.

The White Mountains are a very special place to ski. Bristlecone pines grow there that are over 4,500 years old. The White Mountain uplands are less glaciated and more rolling than the Sierra. If the White Mountain Road is closed near Westgard Pass on Highway 168, it is a long tour up to the Bristlecone groves. Check with the Forest Service in Bishop (619) 873-5841. A tour of into the Whites should be considered an expedition; the range is cold, windy, isolated and beautiful. The University of California maintains a research laboratory near Mt. Bancroft.

There is an excellent alpine tour to Telescope Peak in Death Valley. At 11,000′, Telescope Peak holds snow even though surrounded by the desert. In a wet winter — one with more than a few inches of rain — the barren hillsides of Death Valley National Monument bloom with wildflowers. All Death Valley looks like a giant Persian carpet.

From Trona go north to the Trona Wildrose Highway. Turn right on Wildrose Highway and then right again at the Wildrose Ranger Station (619) 786-2331. You may not be able to drive all the way to Mahogany Flat. Telescope Peak is six miles south. The route follows the summer trail shown on the 15′ Telescope Peak Topo map. Ice axes and crampons should be carried. The route is steep and is often icy, windy and cold.

Bishop Creek Lodge is open in the winter and maintains a track system.

# TOUR 14

**To Piute Pass (11,423' 3482 m)**
**From Camp Sabrina (8960' 2731 m)**
**Mileage: 10 miles 16 km, round trip**
**Elevation Gain: 2563' 781 m**
**Classification: Intermediate alpine; difficult nordic**
**Season: Early March to mid-May**
**Topo Map: *Mt. Goddard***
**Wilderness Permit: Obtain in Bishop**

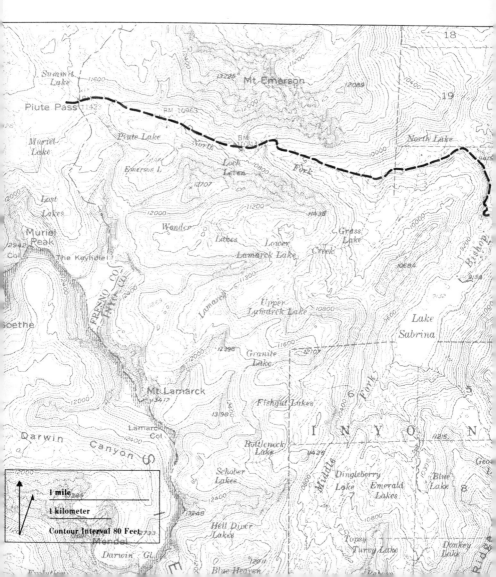

## Features

This tour entices many nordic tourers because it is the first 5 miles of one of the trans-Sierra tours most suitable for nordic skis (Tour 33). It should be made earlier in the year than other tours. The southern exposure of much of the route makes it an early spring tour. Furthermore, there are some excellent ski mountaineering and nordic side tour possibilities in Humphreys Basin which can stretch this tour to three or four days. The wind has been known to blow in this area; be prepared.

## Description

Check out with the Forest Service in Bishop. In Bishop turn west on Highway 168 and drive up to Camp Sabrina. If the road is closed at Camp Sabrina, you will have to hike the easy 1½ miles up to North Lake; the last ½ mile of road before North Lake is dangerous during high avalanche hazard.

From the campground at the roadend work your way roughly west up the north fork of Bishop Creek. The mixture of aspen and lodgepole can be quite bothersome to climb through. Some skiers prefer to ski up along the north ridge of the timber below rust-colored, granitic Mt. Emerson.

After a little over 2 miles the timber virtually ends, and you find youself at the base of a high granite step in the valley floor. Loch Leven Lake lies atop this step. In the small basin below the lake is the last good campsite. The timber here offers shelter from the ever-present wind, and water is sometimes available.

From the campsite, climb to Loch Leven Lake by going up to the right and then traversing to the left (west), coming out just above the lake's outlet. This small cliff area and perhaps the last few feet below Piute Pass are the only parts of the tour where a careless tourer could trigger an avalanche. Ski across the lake and make your way up the middle of the wide canyon, passing isolated stands of wind-battered whitebark pines. Piute Pass will come into sight in the west.

There is a small cabin below Piute Lake that belongs to the California State Department of Water Resources. If you see ski tracks, they might be those of snow surveyors making their rounds. Surveyors usually visit the windswept course near Summit Lake, just over Piute Pass, several times during the spring. Much of the snow just below the pass is a large "snow pillow," deposited when the wind blowing over the pass slows down.

# TOUR 15

To Lamarck Col (13,000′ 3962 m)
From North Lake (9380′ 2859 m)
Mileage: 11 miles 18 km, round trip
Elevation Gain: 3620′ 1103 m
Classification: Difficult alpine
Season: Mid-May to mid-June
Topo Map: *Mt. Goddard*
Wilderness Permit: Obtain in Bishop

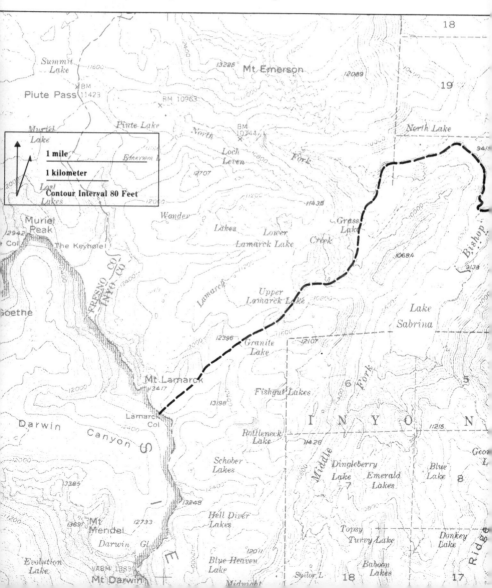

## Features

The tour to Lamarck Col has long been a favorite of ski mountaineers. The descent is a long, continuous run to the North Lake campground. This tour has been done as a very long day tour, but most skiers will find it more enjoyable if they take two days. Choose a time when the sun is shining, softening the snow so the edges of your skis will bite.

## Description

For driving directions see Tour 14. From the campground at the roadend, follow the stream until you reach a footbridge. Cross the stream and go up the creek draining the Lamarck Lakes. In low snow years you will be able to follow the Lamarck Lakes trail. After 1½ miles, turn left (south). Less than ¾ mile ahead is Grass Lake. Grass Lake is in a late stage of ecological succession: now a swamp, it will eventually become a meadow and later a lodgepole flat.

A good campsite will be found on the north shore of Grass Lake. The campsite and the route to it are in timber, with little threat from wind or avalanche.

From the south end of the lake, ascend a 300', heavily wooded slope to a series of cliffs. Turn right and traverse along the cliff base for ¼ mile to a gully leading up toward an open slope. Turn left and climb 800' up this gully; then cross to the right above a rocky bench, where water is sometimes available.

Above the bench continue up, keeping to the right and crossing above a snowcourse. Above the snow marker you lose 50' while traversing into a broad gully. Follow this gully to a large cirque with a flat floor. Lamarck Col is the first col to the right of the prominent spire in the arete south of Mt. Lamarck. Climb 300' up a steep couloir to Lamarck Col (13,000'). If there is enough snow, you can climb on skis up the southeast face nearly to the summit of Mt. Lamarck.

# TOUR 16

**To Saddlerock Lake (11,000′ 3353 m)**
**From South Lake (9755′ 2973 m)**
**Mileage: 8 miles 13 km round trip**
**Elevation Gain: 1250′ 381 m**
**Classification: Intermediate alpine: the Bishop Pass option is
  intermediate-to-difficult nordic**
**Season: April or later**
**Topo Map:** *Mt. Goddard*
**Wilderness Permit: Obtain in Bishop**

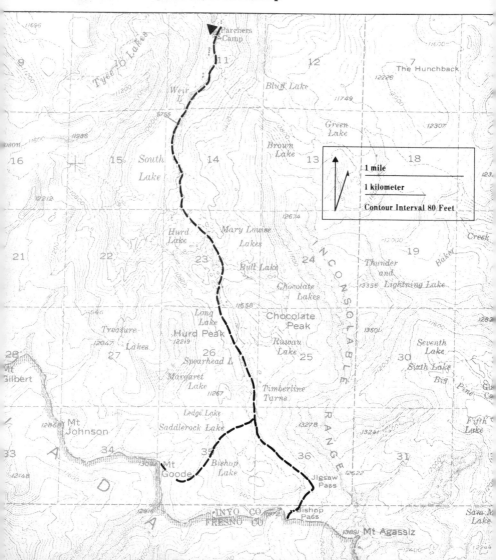

## Features

Experienced nordic tourers can cross Bishop Pass to Dusy Basin to savor winter in the high country while negotiating relatively easy alpine terrain. If you plan to visit Dusy Basin, study weather reports carefully so that you don't end up spending all your time watching a storm from inside your tent.

Alpine tourers will enjoy climbing Mt. Goode (13,092'). You can climb almost to the summit blocks on skis. Compared with nearby ski ascents, the climb is not very difficult.

## Description

Turn west on Highway 168 in Bishop. Drive as far as possible up the South Lake road. During a big snow year you might have to ski a few miles up the road to South Lake. Many high-country roads are not plowed until just before fishing season, when the local resorts are about to open.

From the roadend at South Lake, climb south toward Hurd Peak. During some low snow years you will have to carry your skis the first ½ mile. After about 1 mile, when the slope lessens somewhat, veer east. The route more or less follows the summer trail. Climb past Timberline Tarns to Saddlerock Lake, where you can make camp. There is often water, and wood is available.

The climb from Saddlerock Lake to Bishop Pass (12,000') is very easy. On this climb, remember that gullies, with their narrow bottoms and steep sides, can easily bury an unwary skier who only has eyes for the large and obvious avalanche chutes on the high ridges.

To climb Mt. Goode, starting from the campsite, cross Saddlerock Lake and ski up the steep southeast-facing slope to the summit blocks. Remove your skis and walk to the summit. There are a few whitebark pines up to 11,500' that help protect a skier from wind and sun. In good weather this is an excellent tour, providing a ski mountaineer with a long, steep run back to the lake.

# TOUR 17

To Treasure Lake (10,650′ 3246 m)
From South Lake (9755′ 2973 m)
Mileage: 6 miles 10 km, round trip
Elevation Gain: 900′ 274 m
Classification: Intermediate alpine
Season: Early April to mid-May
Topo Map: *Mt. Goddard*
Wilderness Permit: Obtain in Bishop

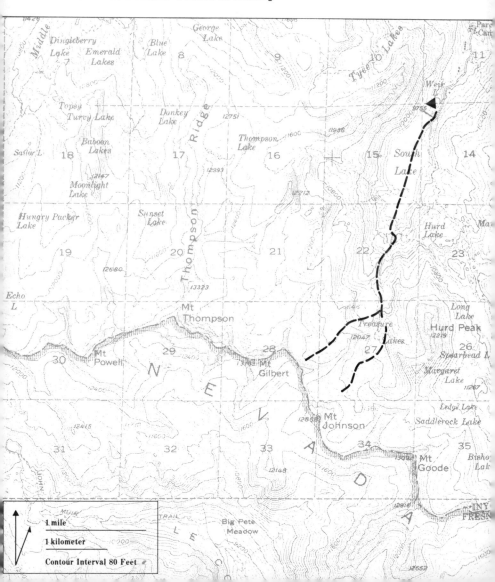

## Features

This tour can be done in one long day, but many skiers make an overnight tour of it, climbing Mt. Gilbert on the second day. Except when crossing South Lake, the tour to Treasure Lakes is through moderately dense timber. The large bowls above Treasure Lakes offer some of the best runs in the area.

You must ski several additional miles if the road has not been plowed to the lake. Avoid this tour when there is any avalanche hazard.

## Description

Check out with the Forest Service in Bishop. Drive west from Bishop on Highway 168 to South Lake; you may have to park some way below the lake. Ski across South Lake to its south end, avoiding inlets, where the ice may be thin. Climb the slope west of the stream that drains Treasure Lakes. Stay on the west side of the stream and work your way, roughly south, to Lower Treasure Lake. As you climb to the lakes, lodgepole is always present and fir is occasionally in evidence.

To climb Mt. Gilbert, ski southwest from Lower Treasure Lake and ascend the slope below the col east of Mt. Gilbert. The climb is steep. You will have to leave your skis at about 12,000', and you will need an ice axe, crampons and possibly other mountaineering equipment.

Instead of climbing to the summit, you may prefer to ski the cirques below Mt. Gilbert. There are several bowls, all of which offer good spring skiing. The snow holds well in the bowls between Mt. Gilbert and Mt. Johnson. In early morning, the sun softens its surface, and in the afternoon, the sun sets behind the Sierra crest. There is usually snow in the bowls when other areas are bare.

# TOUR 18

To Kearsarge Pass (11,800′ 3597 m)
From Onion Valley (9100′ 2774 m)
Mileage: 6 miles 10 km, round trip
Elevation Gain: 2700′ 823 m
Classification: Intermediate alpine
Season: Early March through April
Topo Maps: *Mt. Pinchot, Mt. Whitney*
Wilderness Permit: Obtain in Bishop or Lone Pine

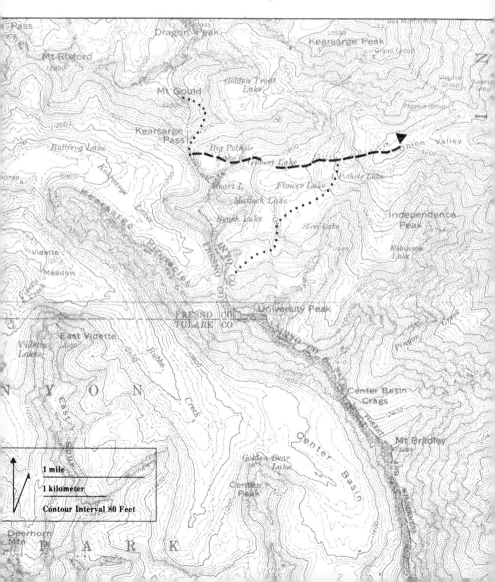

## Features

Experienced nordic skiers, as well as alpine skiers, will enjoy
the tour over Kearsarge Pass. We describe the route only as
far as the pass, but from there, there are many possibilities for
the adventurous. For example, alpine skiers can ski up to
within 600' of the summit of Mt. Gould, or ascend the cirque
north of University Peak.

## Description

From Independence drive west on the Onion Valley Road.
From the end of the road, roughly follow the trail that climbs
to the west. In certain snow conditions, firm corn snow, for instance, you can ski up the slope on a much more direct line than
the switchbacking trail follows. Skirt the north shores of
Flower and Gilbert lakes. Climb moderately, then steeply to an
overlook above the north shore of Big Pothole Lake. The route
up to within 800' of Kearsarge Pass is forested and relatively
free of avalanche paths.

From Kearsarge Pass you can climb northeast, curving up
around Mt. Gould and eventually reaching its summit from the
east. You will have to walk the last 600' to the summit.

This tour is in the sun from early morning on, and there may be
some bare spots late in the spring. If the snow is too shallow,
an alternative tour leaves the main tour about 1 mile from the
roadend and heads southwest up a canyon, crossing Matlock
Lake. Ski southwest until you pass Slim Lake. From the lake,
climb west up a steep slope to a low point on a rocky ridge.
Then follow the southeast side of the ridge until you can
traverse into a large basin which holds a small, unnamed lake.
Alpine skiers will enjoy the skiing in this basin, which has a
perfect exposure and good snow.

# TOUR 19

To Mt. Whitney (14,495′ 4418 m)
From Whitney Portal (8360′ 2548 m)
Mileage: 21 miles 34 km, round trip
Elevation Gain: 6135′ 1870 m
Classification: Difficult alpine
Season: Mid-March through April
Topo Maps: *Lone Pine, Mt. Whitney*
Wilderness Permit: Obtain in Bishop or Lone Pine

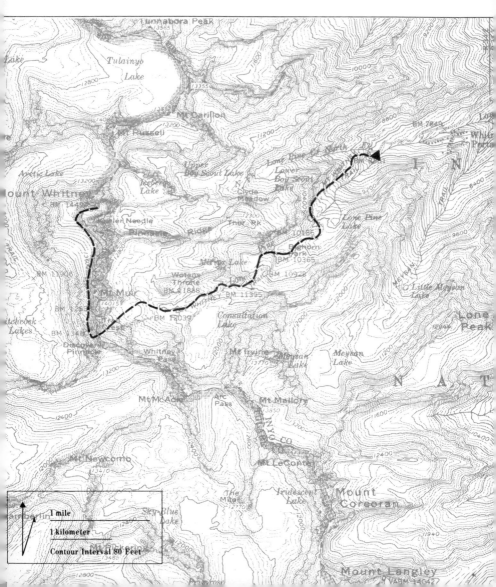

# Features

Most peaks in the Sierra force a skier to remove his or her skis for at least the last few hundred feet, but the tour to the highest point in the contiguous United States can be made on skis all the way up.

This tour crosses several life zones because of the change in elevation. Varying snow conditions will be encountered on most ascents, except perhaps in early winter, when the whole tour takes place in arctic conditions.

Whitney was first climbed on skis using the route described here by Dr. F. Zwickey in March 1929. Each year several parties attempt the ski ascent; in addition, a few mountaineering parties ski up to the high cirques and climb one of the routes on Whitney's east face.

The weather is changeable and tricky. Weeks of balmy weather can be followed by weeks of cold, when windy storms make travel dangerous and difficult. What looks like a collection of small white clouds on the Whitney crest, seen from Lone Pine, is a howling blizzard to skiers trying to find their way up to the summit.

The complete tour usually takes three days. Many ski touring parties make the climb to Trail Crest (13,777') in two days. Take a few days' extra food and don't hesitate to turn back or sit out a storm.

In the quiet and solitude up the canyon and along the crest, it is hard to imagine the traffic jams that occur on the trail in summer. Ski tourers should use their best wilderness manners: avoid campfires (illegal here now), carry out all garbage, camp where summer hikers are not likely to.

## Description

From Lone Pine drive up the Whitney Portal road to its end. The tour follows the trail to the 12,000' level. The first 2 miles of the route ascend a sunny slope. During low snow years you might have to carry your skis here. After the first 2 miles, the route is more shaded.

Once past Lone Pine Lake, climb 300' in ½ mile to Bighorn Park (also called Outpost Camp), just under 10,000', where there are several good campsites with water and shelter. From Bighorn Park our route follows the trail up a steep 400' rise past Mirror Lake. Thor Peak's granite wall and Pinnacles Ridge lend an alpine feeling to this stretch. Then the route turns west toward Mt. Whitney, climbing a moderate slope north of Consultation Lake.

Photo: Marshall Crossman

At 12,500′ leave the summer trail and continue west-northwest for ½ mile. Then turn southwest and work your way up the wide, steep slope to Trail Crest.

Unstable snow can last a long time on this slope. If the snow is wind-packed and sounds hollow when walked or skied on, or there is no resistance when you push your ski pole plus your arm into the snow, an avalanche hazard exists. The slope is always hazardous for at least several days after a snowfall.

At Trail Crest turn north and ski or walk along the crest to the summit. In a few places you will have to drop below the trail, losing elevation. If dark clouds appear in the west, turn back. Storms come up quickly, always bringing gusty, high winds, cold, and poor visibility.

**West Side of the Sierra**

## TOURING AREA: Bear Valley and Pinecrest

During the winter of 1906-07, 73½ feet of snow fell at Tamarack near Bear Valley, a record for the Sierra. Most winters you can count on ample snow and good skiing in the area. Calaveras Big Trees State Park is on Highway 4, the road to Bear Valley.

There are two nordic ski centers in the Bear Valley area; one at **Tamarack Lodge (209) 753-2594** located two miles before the Bear Valley Lodge, and the Bear Valley Nordic Ski School (209) 753-2844 located in Bear Valley Lodge. Every March the Lodge's ski center sponsors the 15 kilometer Bjornloppet Race. Both centers have tours to back-country huts. There is a touring trail system marked with yellow triangles on the south side of the road. There are trailheads at Tamarack and across Highway 4 at Bear Valley. The ski tour up Highway 4 toward Lake Alpine and Ebbetts Pass is good providing snowmobiles haven't made the road unskiable. The Big Meadow 15′ topo covers most of this area.

Highway 108 is closed just a few miles beyond Pinecrest. Pinecrest is the closest ski touring area to San Francisco. When the snow is good the beach at Pinecrest Lake is a very good beginner area. Stay off the lake; the ice on it is always thin. The snowed-in Sonora Pass road is very popular with snowmobilers. The best nordic skiing in the area is up toward the Dodge Ridge ski resort.

Take the road to the ski resort and park just before you come to the one-way loop. Overnight parking is not allowed on the loop or resort parking lot. There are two trail heads. The trails are marked with standard United States Forest Service blue diamond ski trail markers. The Crabtree trailhead is to the south of the loop intersection. About ¼ mile down the trail you will come to a trail signboard at an intersection of two ski trails. Novice skiers will have the best skiing if they go right to the Experimental Forest. The forest has some excellent stands of ponderosa pine and incense cedar. There is also a large clear-cut at the experimental forest that is popular with nordic downhillers. At the trail intersection if you turn left onto the snow-covered Crabtree road in 2½ miles you will come to Aspen Meadow then to Burst Rock and back by way of the Gooseberry Road—a long day tour. Advanced skiers often ski out and back on the Gooseberry Road. The snow is good and you can see from Bear Valley to the Clark Range. Some skiers say that they can see Pyramid Peak near Tahoe from viewpoints on the road. Weather Station, a short ridge which is the high-point on the Crabtree-Gooseberry Loop, is a good day tour for better skiers. Tour parties have had close calls with avalanches near Powell Lake.

Wilderness Permits are required beyond Burst Rock where the Emigrant Wilderness begins. Information and permits may be obtained at Summit Ranger Station (209) 965-3434 to the left at the Dodge Ridge turn-off. Sonora Mountaineering (209) 532-5621 has a complete rental department, maps and up-to-date trail information. It is located in the Mono Village Center off Hillsdale Drive a few miles east of Sonora on Highway 108.

## TOURING AREA: Tuolumne Meadows

There is a park ranger at the Tuolumne Ranger Station most of the winter. The meadows are a meeting point for trans-Sierra tours over Donohue, Mono and Tioga Passes. Nordic tourers will have no problem finding tours in the meadows and forests near the Tuolumne River. When the Tioga Road is plowed there are usually several weeks of skiing before the snow melts. (The road has been snowed-in by late storms after it was plowed, so be prepared to make a hasty retreat.)

To learn what happens within a snowpack, study the snowbanks along the road. Snowbanks along highways that are open all year are disturbed by repeated plowing. The snowbanks along the Tioga Road, when it has been plowed once, are not disturbed. The snow profile—the cross section through the snow, showing its layers—is exposed. The snow on nearby avalanche paths will have similar profiles. If you have kept track of the weather during the year—particularly of the big storms—you can determine which storm each layer came from. A dirty ice layer above a layer of small-grained snow crystals is from a long period of clear weather. If the snow grains are large, the ice layer might be an old rain crust. Look at the lower layers, particularly for differences in hardness and in type of grain. Snow rangers and other snow researchers spend hours digging pits in the snow, but here is an opportunity to observe the snowpack with no such effort. The roadside snowpack is, in effect, a snow pit miles long, a snow transect of the Sierra.

Novice nordic tourers will enjoy Dana Meadows. In certain areas the meadows are just steep enough to practice telemark and other turns. Lyell Canyon offers 8 miles of very skiable nordic terrain.

Farther west down the road, near Tenaya Lake, you may ski  through the ghost forest created by the lodgepole needle-miner. In its two-year pupa stage, this small insect eats the soft inner portion of no more than five pine needles — but there are billions of little lodgepole needleminers. The insect, possibly with the help of the mountain pine beetle, has destroyed thousands of lodgepole pines. The Park Service has sprayed for this member of the Lepidoptera around camp-grounds and along roads to preserve "green belts." However, spraying also kills the predators and parasites of the insect, which are the biological controls that would prevent a resurgence in its population. Hence, in a seeming paradox, spraying that kills insects can produce an eventual *increase* in the insect population. The only way that the lodgepole needle-miner will ever be controlled is through an integrated pro-gram, probably using natural ecological components, such as fire, to remove the old trees. In addition, predators (such as chickadees), insect parasites, and chemicals such as sex attrac-tants will probably be used. The sex attractants keep the male and female from finding each other. There will always be some needle-miners about; they are a part of the complex lodgepole ecosystem.

In addition to the tours described, alpine tourers will enjoy the run down Mt. Hoffman's south bowl. The alpine tour to the summit of Mt. Lyell is a classic. It can be done in two days, but three is more pleasant.

# TOUR 20

To Mt. Dana (13,053′ 3979 m)
From Tioga Pass (9945′ 3031 m)
Mileage: 7 miles 11 km, round trip
Elevation Gain: 3100′ 945 m
Classification: Difficult alpine
Season: Best just after the Tioga Road opens
Topo Maps: *Tuolumne Meadows, Mono Craters*

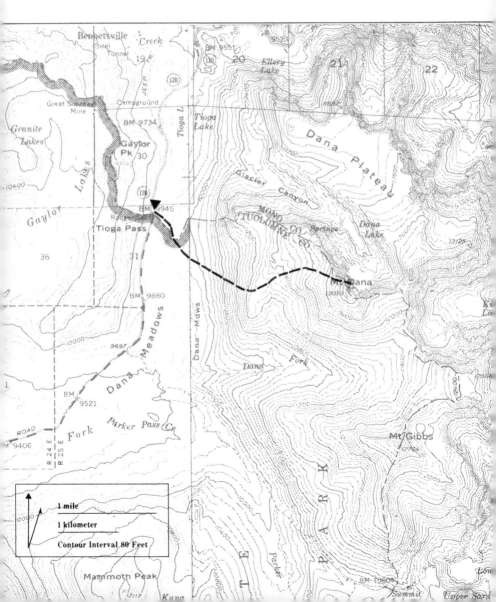

## Features

This is the most popular alpine tour in the Tuolumne region. The view from the summit is most rewarding. From the interior desert ranges in the east to the rolling Tuolumne country at your feet to the west, the scene is spectacular. Timber, wind and sun reign supreme. The entire climb is in the sun most of the day and exposed to the southwest wind. Mountaineers climb on the steep, hanging glacier on the north face of Mt. Dana well into fall.

## Description

Drive to Tioga Pass on Highway 120 and park at the cleared area near the entrance station, where you check out. From the parking area, you can pick out the best route up Mt. Dana, whose base is just across Dana Meadows. If the snow surface is hard, you may have to carry your skis on the steeper portions.

From the parking area, ski southeast across the meadows. When you reach the foot of the mountain, climb due east, traversing your way up the slope. At about 11,400′ the slope tapers off, and it is more gentle until the last 400′ below the summit. Skis are usually left here where it is an easy scramble over rock to the top.

Yosemite high country
Photo: Gordon Wing

## Touring Area: Yosemite Valley and environs

Yosemite National Park offers a great variety of touring areas, particularly around Badger Pass, 15 miles from Yosemite Valley up the Glacier Point road. The tour from Summit Meadow (not named on the topo; 1 mile beyond the Badger Pass ski resort) along the road toward Glacier Point is popular. The touring farther south, in the Mariposa Grove of Big Trees, is enjoyable too. The Sequoias seem even more imposing and regal in winter. Many skiers go to Crane Flat or other areas along the Oak Flat and Tioga Roads.

The Yosemite Mountaineering and Guide School offers instruction, ski rentals and guide service. It was one of the first nordic schools in California, and is still one of the most popular. Hundreds of skiers enter the annual spring cross country race that the school sponsors. Most of the contestants have never raced before; the prevailing spirit is festive rather than seriously competitive.

Yosemite is beginning to be crowded year-round. The Park Service, which has the impossible task of both preserving the Park in its natural form and maintaining it as a source of recreation for large numbers of people, has imposed many regulations that will annoy tourers who are used to freer, less crowded snow country. Perhaps the best solution is to stay away from Yosemite on holidays. Ski trail maps are available at the touring center in the Valley or from the Park Service.

# TOUR 21

**To Dewey Point (7385′ 2251 m)**
**From Summit Meadow (7300′ 2225 m)**
**Mileage: 6 miles 10 km, round trip**
**Classification: Intermediate nordic**
**Season: Early December to late April**
**Topo Map:** *Yosemite*

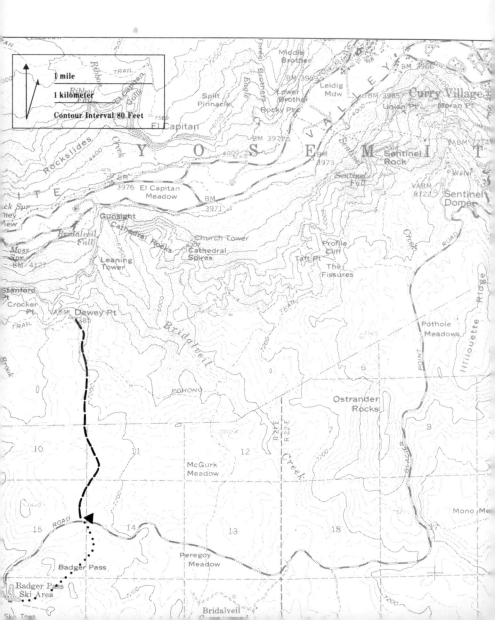

## Features

This nordic tour is the most popular one in Yosemite. The route follows ideal nordic terrain, gentle; rolling slopes with no long, sustained climbs. At the tour's destination, Dewey Point, the skier is rewarded with a view of Yosemite Valley, 3300′ below, and the southeast face of El Capitan, across the Valley. Skiers should take their light skis: this is a tour for traveling light and working on technique. The trail is often packed and the going is easy.

## Description

The starting point of this tour is Summit Meadow, at the end of the plowed portion of the Glacier Point road, 15 miles from Yosemite Valley and 1 mile beyond the Badger Pass ski area. The route starts off north through lodgepole pine, goes northeast through several small meadows and then turns north again. The trail is marked by yellow triangles fastened to trees.

On your return, ski along the rim of Yosemite Valley for a little while before turning south.

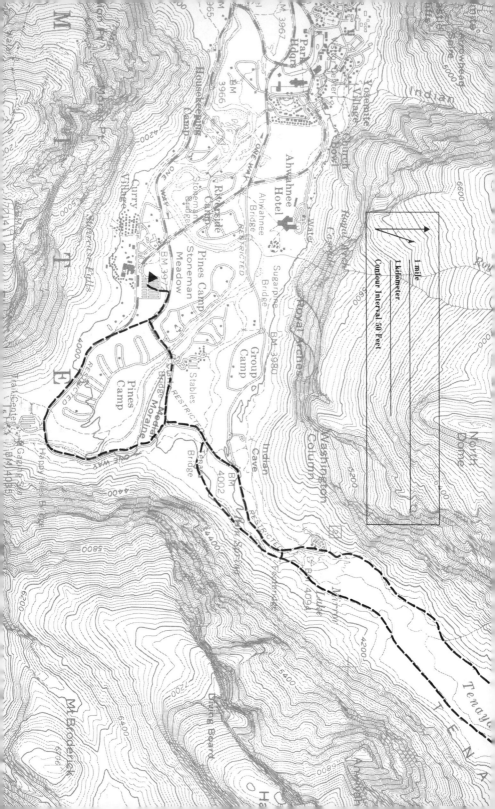

# TOUR 22

To Mirror Lake (4100' 1250 m)
From Camp Curry (4000' 1219 m)
Mileage: 7 miles 11 km, semiloop tour
Elevation Gain: 100' 30 m
Classification: Novice nordic
Season: Early winter or whenever there is snow
  in Yosemite Valley
Topo Map: *Yosemite* or the U.S.G.S. Yosemite Valley
  (scale: 1" = 2000')

## Features

This is a tour for a day when the weather at Badger Pass is
stormy. It is 3000' lower than Badger, in sheltered Yosemite
Valley. It will take you away from automobiles and into the
less developed part of the Valley. Taking a tour like this is one
of the few ways to get some idea of what the Valley was like in
a less hectic era.

If you time this tour for the first warm, sunny day after a large
storm, you will be treated to the sight of avalanches cascading
like waterfalls over the surrounding cliffs. Snow bonds poorly
to the smooth exfoliated granite, and the warm sun releases
avalanches. After a big storm, moreover, you can be confident
that you will find enough snow. At any other time you might
encounter bare spots. During sunny weather the snow will be
variable, so take along a variety of waxes.

Much of the route will have been packed by other skiers,
unless you get an early start. The entire tour follows roads and
bridle paths, and road and trail signs will be visible most of the
time. If you don't want to make the whole tour up to Snow
Creek, cross the bridge below Mirror Lake.

Yosemite Valley
Photo: Gordon Wing

## Description

The tour starts from the Camp Curry parking lot, which is near the east end of Yosemite Valley. From Camp Curry head east, crossing Clarks Bridge. Take the bridle path to the right (east) just before the Tenaya Bridge and ski up the east side of Tenaya Canyon, following snowed-in bridle paths.

Cross Tenaya Creek just before Snow Creek and ski back along the path west of Tenaya Creek and Mirror Lake. From Mirror Lake ski down the road, it will be easier to make turns on it. At Tenaya Bridge you complete your loop. From here, retrace the route back to Camp Curry.

An interesting side tour from Camp Curry is the loop crossing Happy Isles Bridge and Clarks Bridge. Leave the Camp Curry parking lot, and after 100 yards turn southeast on the road that leads to the fish hatchery. Stay on the road, crossing the Merced River on Happy Isles Bridge and then on Clarks Bridge.

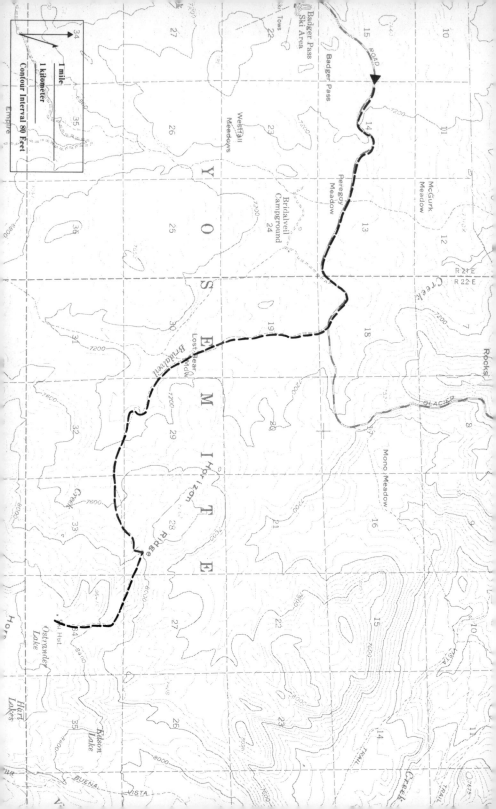

# TOUR 23

To Ostrander Lake (8600' 2621 m)
From Summit Meadow (7300' 2225 m)
Mileage: 18 miles 29 km, round trip
Elevation Gain: 1300' 396 m
Classification: Intermediate-to-difficult nordic
Season: Early January to late April
Topo Map: *Yosemite*

## Features

The tour into Ostrander Lake is one of the classic ones in Yosemite. This tour is usually made on light touring skis, which work very well in the usual snow conditions; however, one might have difficulty skiing with them on old frozen rain crust. Since the hut at the lake is crowded on weekends, the best time to go is during the week.

The first few miles of the tour are along the Glacier Point road, which is a busy thoroughfare for skiers and snowshoers. Once you leave the road, the tour is more secluded, because the route is through timber most of the way. As you ski along, you will have a few enticing views of the High Sierra to the east.

Reservations are necessary for Ostrander Hut. Apply to:

Superintendent, Yosemite National Park
P.O. Box 577
Yosemite National Park, California 95389
(209) 372-4232

For a weekend or a holiday, apply many weeks in advance. There is a $2 a night charge for each person staying in the hut.

From the hut there are several good side tours. Alpine skiers enjoy skiing the bowls below Horse Ridge. Several marked ski trails originate at the hut. In addition to the route described here, skiers can take the Horizon Ridge trail or the Merced Crest trail back from Ostrander Lake. The only avalanche hazard is below the cornices on Horse Ridge.

## Description

You must check out at the Badger Pass Ranger Station. The rangers will tell you where to park and will keep a set of your car keys. (If it storms they will have to move cars around so that the parking lot at the ski area can be plowed).

Drive east on the Glacier Point road past the ski area. Summit Meadow is about 1 mile beyond the ski area. One person will

171

have to drive back to the parking lot. The first mile of the tour takes you along a fairly level road through mixed timber. Then there is a long, gradual run down toward Peregoy Meadow. Although gradual, this run can be very fast; watch for ruts in the snow.

The meadows around here are not as large as they look on the topo map, because lodgepole pines are gradually encroaching. From Peregoy Meadow you can see the Clark Range in the east, and Horizon Ridge and corniced Horse Ridge, in the southeast.

Beyond Peregoy Meadow the road climbs gradually over a low hill. At the base of this hill, just beyond Bridalveil Creek, the Ostrander Lake ski trail to the south begins. From this point the route follows an old jeep trail to Ostrander Lake. A sign beside the road just past the creek shows the route into Ostrander Hut. The sign is readjusted after each storm, so it is visible most of the time.

Often you will have to ski on snowcat tracks make by snow surveyor's vehicles. The route can be difficult to find when there are no tracks. From the road, it winds south for 2 miles, recrossing the creek after ¼ mile, to a point near the west fork of Bridalveil Creek. Then the route follows the creek for ¾ mile before it begins to climb southeast.

Up to this point the tour is a rolling uphill one through dense-to-open lodgepole stands, with some white fir. Wood and sometimes water are available along this stretch of the tour. Those tourers who are prepared to snowcamp and don't want to carry their packs uphill can set up a base camp here. The rest of the route is steeper.

After crossing a particularly large clearing, the route veers north. In a mile or so you will come out on Horizon Ridge. Follow the ridge southeast for a mile, climbing steeply through open mixed timber. The route levels off on a flat bench where there is a snowcourse.

If you have been climbing the narrow tracks left by a snowcat, you will be happy to leave them here. The snowcourse is a good place to get a view of the Clark Range and the High Sierra beyond it. Mt. Starr King, 5 miles away, is the closest prominent feature in the northeast.

From the snowcourse head southwest and sidehill up and around to the west side of Horizon Ridge. After ¾ mile the trail comes out above Ostrander Lake. The hut is immediately below, just above the lake.

There are several alternative routes to and from Ostrander
Hut. You can ski back to Badger Pass along the Merced Crest,
which is marked with yellow triangles bearing the number 16.
From Ostrander Lake this route climbs up Horse Ridge. If the
snow surface isn't icy, you can also ski northwest down
Horizon Ridge to the Glacier Point road, meeting the road
about 1 mile east of Bridalveil Creek. Except for the cliffs
below Horse Ridge, there is little avalanche terrain on this
route. There are some small steep areas where an avalanche
could be triggered: avoid them.

## TOURING AREA: Huntington-Shaver Lakes

Huntington Lake is 65 miles east of Fresno on Highway 168.
Lessons, rentals and trail information are available from Shaver
Summit Ski Rental (209) 841-7792, located in Shaver Lake across
from Angelo's Bakery. Nordic rentals and lessons are also
available at Lake Shore Village at Huntington Lake. Permits
and information are available at the Pine Ridge Ranger Station
(209) 841-3311 in Shaver Lake.

Tamarack is about 10 miles east of Shaver Lake on Highway
168. There are two nordic loop trails into Tamarack and Cutts
Meadows. The trail markers are brown square plates with
white nordic skiers printed on them. The trailheads are at a
small turnout located ½ mile southeast from the Tamarack
Crest parking lot.

Nordic skiers who wish to stretch their legs should try the 10
mile tour around Huntington Lake, starting from China Peak.
The first 4 miles will take you along the relatively undeveloped
south shore. If you don't want to ski near the highway or other
signs of man, turn back at the dam. If you continue around the
lake be careful near the outlet and inlets. Most of the time you
will have to cross the bridges over the inlets and cross the dam
around the outlet.

Intermediate skiers who wish to tour at higher elevations can
buy a ride on the chair lift to the top of China Peak. From the
upper chair lift terminal above 8000′ there are many interesting tours to the south and west on rolling, mostly
timbered uplands. There are many possibilities for longer
tours around Red Mountain. Alpine tourers often ascend the
west ridge of the mountain. If you can arrange transportation,
the nordic tour from the top of the chairlift to Tamarack is
good. The route drops 1500′ in the 5 miles to the lodge. Unless
you enjoy skiing after dark, be sure to allow enough time—
start early.

# TOUR 24

To the Saddle near Luck Point (9300′ 2835 m)
From the Roadend near Huntington Lake (7200′ 2195 m)
Mileage: 10 miles 16 km round trip
Elevation Gain: 1700′ 518 m
Classification: Intermediate nordic
Season: Early January to late April
Topo Map: *Kaiser Peak*

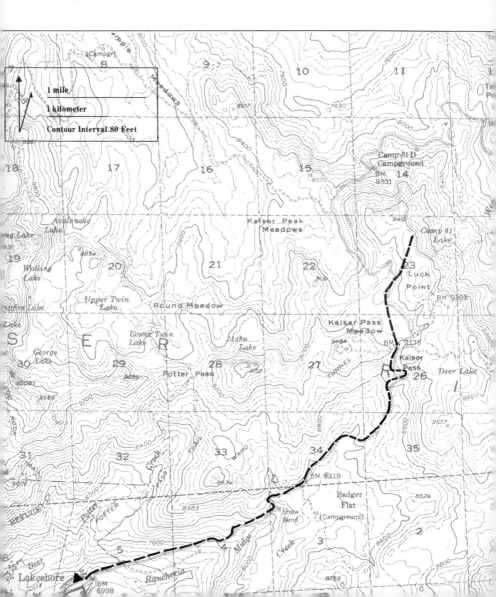

## Features

From Luck Point, near Kaiser Pass, there is a panoramic view of the High Sierra. It includes the south end of the Ritter Range, more than 20 miles northwest; the Silver Divide, about 13 miles northeast; and Mammoth Mountain, which is between True North and Magnetic North.

This tour covers the last 5 miles of a nordic tour over the central Sierra (Tour 33) which goes past Florence Lake (7650´). The lake is 15 miles down the road from Kaiser Pass. But, the slopes on a tour to Florence Lake are nowhere steeper than on the south side of Kaiser Pass, and are fairly level for the last 10 miles. One large avalanche path crosses the road 2 miles north of the pass. Since Florence Lake is lower than Kaiser Pass, it should be visited before the spring thaw. The trans-Sierra tour, going one way, would be almost as short as the round trip to Florence from Lakeshore. Lila Lofberg, in the book *Sierra Outpost*, describes life at Florence Lake during the winter. While maintaining Southern California Edison's facilities, the Lofbergs became interested in the natural history around the outpost. She has some very interesting accounts of mountain coyotes. She fed them each winter and came to know them well.

## Description

Lakeshore is 69 miles east of Fresno on Highway 168. The road to Kaiser Pass starts next to the Ward Tunnel, which, passing under Kaiser Ridge, drains Florence Lake. Depending on snow depth, the tour may start from the Kaiser Pass turnoff at Rancheria Creek, which is 1 mile east of Lakeshore, or several miles up the road.

The road is opened in the spring as soon as possible so that maintenance crews can get to Florence Lake and Lake Thomas A. Edison. In late spring it will be plowed up toward the Rancheria Creek bridge, but it might be closed a mile or so below where it is plowed to. When it is, there is ample snow to ski on beside the road.

The route climbs steadily uphill, contouring alongside Rancheria Creek. Past Rancheria Creek it winds more, and some short sections are moderately steep. For the last ¼ mile before the pass, you might have to side-hill on wind-packed snow. When the snow is deep and rutted by snowcats or snowmobiles, traveling is easier beside the road than on it.

From the pass, ski north. You will cross Kaiser Meadow, pass a snowcourse and come out on the ridge that runs north from Luck Point. This is the best place for a view.

# TOURING AREA:
## Sequoia and Kings Canyon National Parks

In addition to the high country tours that attract ski mountaineers, there are excellent nordic tours in the Sequoia groves and meadows in Sequoia Park. Novice nordic skiers will enjoy the tour along the Crescent Meadow road. At Moro Rock there is an excellent view of the peaks along the Great Western Divide. The road begins on the west side of the restaurant in Giant Forest. Skiing on the first mile of the road is often difficult because many tourists wade through the snow to Moro Rock. Crescent Meadow is 1½ miles farther. Novice skiers who want to ski through the Sequoia groves leave Crescent Meadow and ski 2 miles northwest, following a touring trail marked with yellow triangles to Circle Meadow and then head north to the road. The tour may be made in the other direction. Novice skiers can ski a short way into the Sequoias by skiing out to Sunset Rock. There is a touring center in Giant Forest where you may have instruction and rent skis.

Wolverton is a small ski area with rope tows three miles north of Giant Forest. There are good places to practice downhill turns plus a long meadow where you can practice diagonal stride. It is a good place for children. About 1½ miles north of Wolverton at Lodgepole the Park Service maintains a campground in winter. They also offer programs on Saturday evenings.

The Park Service has natural history ski tours and ski trails; check at the visitor centers in Lodgepole and Grant Grove. There is a self guided orienteering trail near the General Sherman Tree.

If the General's Highway is open, you will find good tours in Big Meadows, 20 miles beyond Giant Forest. The Park Service has a marked touring trail along Big Baldy Ridge. During winters of heavy snowfall, the General's Highway is not plowed beyond the Marble Fork of the Kaweah River.

One hundred yards south of the Baldy Ridge trailhead is the Big Meadows road turn-off. The four mile tour into the meadows is one of the most pleasant tours in the Sequoia Kings Canyon area. If the road is too tracked by snowmobiles there is a trail that parallels it on its south side. The trail is marked by blue diamonds.

Montecito Sequoia (415) 967-8612 is a touring lodge with some services. Its access road is located ½ mile to the south of Baldy Ridge. Wilsonia Ski Touring (209) 335-2404 is located in Wilsonia near Grant Grove. They offer rentals, lessons and tours into huts.

# TOUR 25

To Pear Lake (9500′ 2896 m)
From the Wolverton Ski Area Parking Lot (7200′ 2195 m)
Mileage: 12 miles 19 km, round trip
Elevation Gain: 2300′ 701 m
Classification: Moderate alpine, difficult nordic
Season: Early January through April
Topo Map: *Triple Divide Peak*

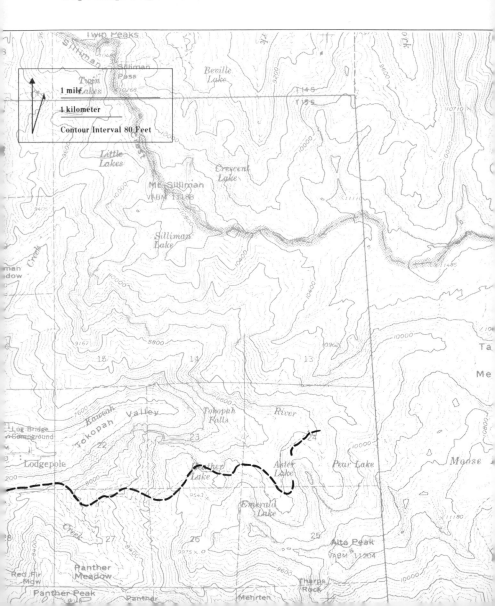

# Features

This tour which leads to the Pear Lake Hut is the most popular alpine tour in Sequoia National Park. Pear Lake makes an excellent base camp for skiing on Alta Peak or exploring the Tablelands. The route is relatively free of avalanche paths.

The Pear Lake Hut was built by the Civilian Conservation Corps between 1936 and 1939 to serve skiers. In those days there were no lifts and there was little distinction between alpine and nordic skiing. For weekends and holidays, hut reservations must be made months ahead. Make reservations with:

Sequoia Natural History Association
Sequoia and Kings Canyon National Parks
Three Rivers, CA 93271
Phone: (209) 565-3341

The hut sleeps 10 (more in a pinch). It has an oil-burning heater and gas cookstoves and lamps. First-aid and avalanche rescue gear are also kept in the hut.

Pear Lake suffers excessive summer impact. Don't use campfires at Pear Lake; camp in out-of-the-way spots.

# Description

From the Park headquarters (about 2 miles inside the Park on Highway 198) drive east on the General's Highway. The turnoff to Wolverton is 3 miles past Giant Forest.

From the middle of the northern parking lot at Wolverton, climb northeast for 100 yards. If the snow is not too deep, the well-used summer trail will be visible. You come out on a low, modest ridge which angles up to the northeast almost 1 mile up the ridge.

The route is marked with yellow triangles on trees. It is heavily traveled during weekends and holidays, but one might still get lost on the first half (3 miles) of the tour up to Heather Gap.

The ridge, which separates the small Wolverton Creek drainage from the larger Marble Fork of the Kaweah River, ends in a steep hillside. Sidehill southwest up the steep hill. After ¼ mile the route turns up the hill, leaving the summer trail. Switchback up the steep hillside through a long clearing, always going in a generally eastward direction.

As you climb, you will get an occasional glimpse of the hills surrounding Wolverton. Various pines begin to appear, with Jeffrey predominating. After a mile, the second half of which is along a moderate swale formed by one of the branches of

Pear Lake Hut

Wolverton Creek, the grade lessens. Continue upward, bearing more to the northeast. One-half mile farther a bumpy snowfield is visible across a small gully. The bumps are large granite boulders covered with snow. Heather Gap is not far beyond the field. The scenery becomes alpine at this point.

If you leave the main tour route at Heather Gap and follow the top of the buttress ½ mile north, you will arrive at the Watch Tower, a 1000′ cliff more the realm of rock climbers than skiers. The whole area around Tokopah Falls is steep; don't try to ski down it. Looking east past the main route, you can see the ridge dropping from Alta Peak which separates the Aster Lake basin from the Pear Lake basin.

From Heather Gap, sacrifice 200′ and ski down to Heather Lake; it's faster than trying to sidehill on the steep slope above the lake, and safer if there is any avalanche hazard. Cross the lake and cilmb up the short hillside on its east shore. Follow the natural bench, which leads to a point where you can look down on Aster Lake.

Work your way around the cirque, losing some elevation at small cliffs. Then sidehill upward at a moderate angle toward a small clump of foxtail pines on the hillside north of you.

If you have climbed at a steep enough angle, your rewards, when you arrive at the ridge, will be an exceptional view and a short run down to the hut. When the Central Valley is covered with radiation fog, tourers in the Sierra can look west over a fluffy sea of fog to the Santa Lucia Range along the coast. The hut is located on Pear Creek about a hundred yards up stream of its confluence with the Marble Fork of the Kaweah River. If you plan to camp at Pear Lake, traverse uphill southeast to the lake.

# TOUR 26

**To Giant Forest (6500′ 1981 m)**
**From Wolverton Ski Area Parking Lot (7200′ 2195 m)**
**Mileage: 4 miles 6 km, shuttle tour**
**Elevation Gain: 500′ 152 m; loss 1100′ 335 m**
**Classification: Novice alpine or intermediate nordic**
**Season: Mid-January through March**
**Topo Maps: *Triple Divide Peak, Giant Forest***

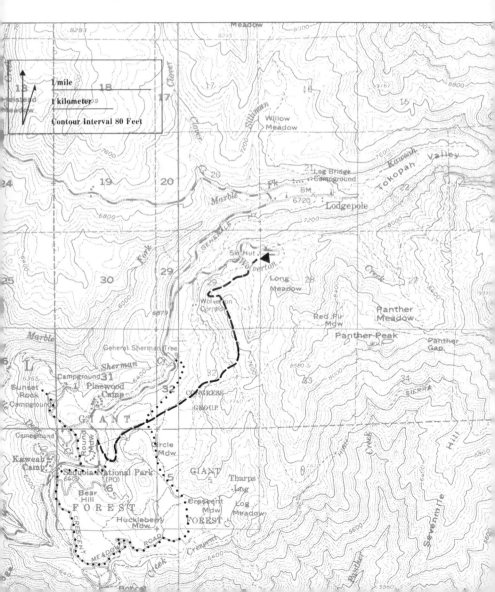

## Features

Touring through a Sequoia grove affects you in an odd way. It  is always quiet. The snow covers all the small features such as rocks and bushes. There is nothing but the snow, yourself, and those giant trees.

At the end of this tour, one of your party will have to go back for the car at Wolverton, or else someone must drive down to meet you.

## Description

From Giant Forest in Sequoia National Park drive east on the General's Highway. Turn right after 3 miles to Wolverton, the small ski resort is 1½ miles farther in.

The Park Service has marked the route with yellow triangles. From the parking lot at Wolverton, ski southwest to the top of the highest rope tow at the left of the shallow gully. Follow the trail markers west.

After passing some large sugar pines, the route begins to sidehill up at a slight angle. Whenever you find sugar pines, you can be pretty sure that the forest in the area will be a mix of firs, cedars and various pines. Sugar pine rarely occurs in pure stands. Keep sidehilling up, winding through some small gullies, for ¾ mile. Then the slope opens a little and the route turns south, switchbacking up a steep slope to a ridge.

Along here you pass several tall pines whose lower trunks are blackened by a fire, probably one started by lightning. Fire is a natural part of the local forest ecosystem. By putting out most fires, man has prevented fire from playing its natural role. The species of trees have consequently changed. The old trees here are red firs and Sequoias: most of the saplings are white firs or cedars. Fire used to supply the clearings and mineral soil that Sequoia and red fir need to germinate. Lack of fire also allows the duff and other fuel to accumulate so that a fire, when it finally occurs, is devastating. The thick bark of a Sequoia protects the tree against an "average" fire. The Park Service in Sequoia is now experimenting with "prescribed" burns, hoping to generate more Sequoia seedlings and prevent big fires.

Ski south along the ridge, passing an occasional Jeffrey pine. During warm weather, chickaree tracks are everywhere here. Chickarees fell pine and fir cones and then descend to collect them, leaving a maze of tracks in the snow. Looking west, you can see the tall, rounded crowns of the Sequoia trees along the Marble Fork of the Kaweah. To the east you have an occasional glimpse down to Long Meadow.

After ½ mile the ridge ends and the route drops down to the right (southwest). At first the run down the moderate slope passes through dense timber, but soon the forest opens a little and the slope lessens. At this point you enter Sequoia groves. As long as you have a compass, there will be no route finding problems from here to Giant Forest. Always ski to the southwest, unless you want to find the road, in which case turn northwest. You will come to a trail fork; turn left to Crescent Meadow, right to the Sherman Tree and the road and straight ahead to Giant Forest. The ski trail continues southwest for 1½ miles. The slope is gentle except for the last ½ mile where you will have to ski down a steep, narrow trail. The marked trail turns northwest for the last ¼ mile to Giant Forest.

Putting on skins

To Mineral King Valley (7900' 2408 m) (with side trips)
From the Mineral King Road at Redwood Creek (5600' 1707 m)
Mileage: 20 miles 32 km, round trip
Elevation Gain: 2300' 701 m
Classification: Novice-to-intermediate nordic
Season: Mid-January to late March
Topo Map: *Mineral King*

## Features

The tour up the Mineral King road starts near the top of the chaparral zone and climbs through several plant associations to narrow, glaciated Mineral King Valley. After years of controversy, Mineral King is now part of Sequoia National Park.

Mineral King is well known for avalanches. During the silver mining days, only one person was killed by an avalanche, because the miners spent much of the winter lower down in Silver City. Most of the early mining buildings were located at the bases of avalanche paths on Empire Mountain, and all that remain today are a few cornerstones and ore buckets scattered among the sagebrush. In February 1969 there was another fatality, when an avalanche buried a cabin near the old Mineral King store. There are no safe tours in Mineral King when an avalanche hazard exists. Since the temperatures along the higher ridges and couloirs are often quite low, avalanche hazards may persist for long periods.

In addition to the two alpine tours described below (Tours 28 and 29), there are many more that use the valley as a base camp. Since most of the bowls are hanging valleys, the first few hundred feet into any of them is steep. The tour up to Glacier Pass can provide an excellent run down on a cold, cloudy day. Franklin Bowl is very alpine, lying under the imposing northwest face of Florence Peak and surrounded by high aretes.

## Description

You may check out at the Park headquarters in Ash Mountain. The Mineral King road turns off Highway198 just east of Three Rivers, a few miles west of the entrance to Sequoia National Park. The road climbs rapidly. At the height of a "usual" snow year, you can drive only as far as Redwood Creek, where there are two large Sequoias in the middle of the road, but you

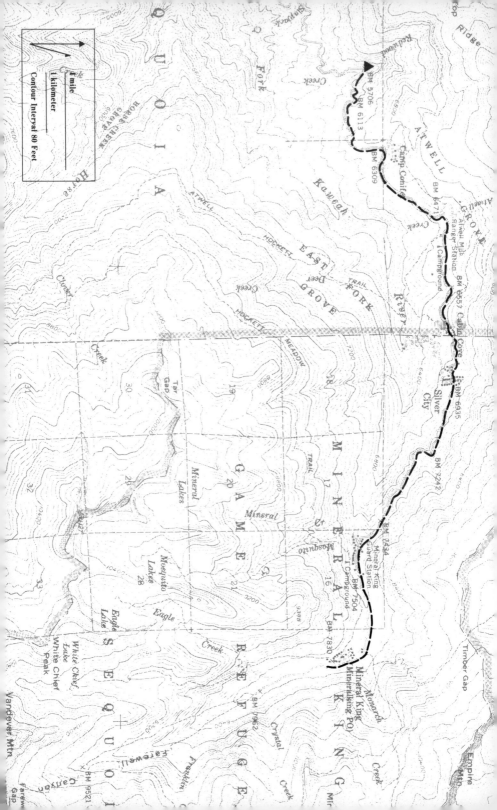

will often be able to park higher. Be sure to park so that you can get back down the road if it snows. There are often snowdrifts and muddy areas above Redwood Creek which become impassable after a thaw or a few inches of snow.

The route winds upward from Redwood Creek, passing through incense cedar and Jeffrey pine. The longest sustained steep section of the tour is the first few miles. Along the road are a few Sequoias. Near Atwell Mill, 6 miles from Mineral King Valley, they become more common. There are several large Sequoia stumps along the road, reminders of the days when the Atwell sawmill was active.

The Silver City Store and cabins are closed in winter. Silver City, where the miners wintered during the silver rush, lies ½ mile from Cabin Cove. The mixed forest along the road includes tall sugar pines, whose extremely long, pendent cones hang from the tips of the sweeping branches.

A mile beyond Silver City the road begins to cut through a steep hillside. The road maintains a moderate grade, but the cliffs at the right are quite steep. In places you can see down canyon to the East Fork of the Kaweah River. Across the canyon, high cirques are visible. Sequoia groves extend from the river almost to the ridge; the Sequoias standing out from the rest of the timber by virtue of their rounded crowns and great height. During the spring runoff, you can hear the falls below Faculty Flat up the canyon.

Several large avalanche paths cross the road between Silver City and Faculty Flat. Look for trees that have some branches or bark missing, the results of avalanche burn. At Faculty Flat the road nears the East Fork of the Kaweah. From here to the end of the valley there are a number of places to camp. Firewood, however, is not abundant anywhere in this heavily visited valley. Above Faculty Flat, leave the forest and climb the gradually sloping road to the main bend in the river, passing some old cottonwoods. Beyond this bend you get the early morning sun. The Mineral King post office and store, shown on the map, was destroyed by avalanches in 1969.

Farther up the canyon are campsites that make good base camps for side trips. You can tour on nordic skis up the valley as far as Franklin Creek. Beyond there, the terrain steepens.

# TOUR 28

To Tulare Peak (11,400′ 3475 m)
From Mineral King Valley (7900′ 2408 m)
Mileage: 7 miles 11 km, round trip
Elevation Gain: 3500′ 1067 m
Classification: Difficult alpine
Season: Early April through May
Topo Map: *Mineral King*

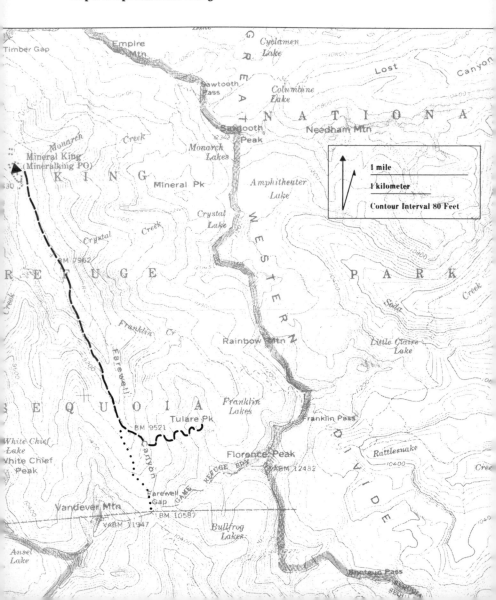

## Features

The run down from the saddle south of Tulare Peak is one of the best in Mineral King. You don't often find good skiing on west slopes, but the snow holds well on this high west bowl. The south side of the bowl is sheltered from the late afternoon sun.

Once out of the timber, you will have no protection from sun or wind, so be prepared. The upper slopes avalanche often. A tour to Farewell Gap is intermediate alpine. Novice nordic skiers will find the Farewell Gap slopes steep.

## Description

For driving directions, see Tour 27. Ski to the south end of the Mineral King Valley. One and one-half miles from Mineral King, cross the East Fork of the Kaweah River to the west bank and climb Aspen Flat's gentle slopes. Aspen Flat is bordered on the west by the creek draining White Chief Bowl, on the east by Franklin Creek.

Past the flat, continue up a moderate slope through mixed timber to a long, narrow clearing at the base of a steep slope. Go left (east) until a draw appears. The trail shown on the west slope of Farewell Canyon on the topo goes up the draw. Climb up the open draw. At first narrow and steep, after ¼ mile the draw levels off. The main drainage of Farewell Canyon is a steep-sided avalanche ravine. Continue up the open draw for 1 mile, always climbing the moderate slope, to an isolated stand of timber. Except for this small stand, avalanches keep Farewell Canyon free of timber. Head for Farewell Gap, which is prominent and obvious.

After climbing ½ mile past the timber, climb to the east. The high saddle south of Tulare Peak will be obvious. From the saddle you will be able to look across the south rim of Franklin Bowl to the 12,000′ northwest face of Florence Peak. The bowl below Rainbow Mountain, to the northeast, will provide good skiing for those who are willing to climb it. When skiing down Tulare Bowl, stay on the south side if there are any exposed rocks directly below the peak.

# TOUR 29

To White Chief Pass (10,800′ 3292 m)
From Mineral King Valley (7900′ 2408 m)
Mileage: 8 miles 13 km, round trip
Elevation Gain: 2900′ 884 m
Classification: Intermediate alpine or difficult nordic
Season: Late March through April
Topo Map: *Mineral King*

## Features

This tour goes to one of the few passes over the Mineral King crest that leads to Hockett Meadows. Experienced nordic skiers can climb up White Chief Pass to ski the 10-mile downhill run to Tar Gap and back to Mineral King via Mineral Bowl and Mosquito Bowl. Only experienced nordic skiers should attempt the loop tour, and then only in years when the snowpack is deep enough. You will be able to tell whether the loop tour is possible when you look toward Hocket Meadows from the pass.

If you tour up White Chief Bowl and then ski down by way of Eagle and Mosquito lakes, you will have skied much of the terrain of a proposed ski resort.

Alpine skiers will enjoy this tour; White Chief Bowl provides good skiing. From White Chief Peak, an easy climb from the pass, you can see Kaweah Peaks, lined up in the northeast, the Tablelands, in the north, and even some of the peaks south of Mt. Whitney on the main Sierra crest, in the east.

## Description

For driving directions, see Tour 27. White Chief Bowl is a hanging valley. The best way to get into it is to follow the route described in Tour 28 until you are 100 yards above the steep portion of Farewell Draw. Turn right (west) and enter the fir forest, sidehilling on a very steep slope. Sidehill up across it at a moderate (10%) grade until you arrive at a narrow bench. Follow this bench for a short distance, until you can turn south.

Work your way up a series of benches with short, sometimes steep climbs between them. After ½ mile a dry lake comes into view as you round a hill. Dry Lake is dry because water there drains into subterranean limestone caverns. Large, very old tree trunks are scattered around the meadow. Apparently a large avalanche swept them down from the bare slopes west of the lake many years ago. Some of the trunks are more than three feet thick. It is a mystery how the trees were able to grow so large before an avalanche removed them.

Ski toward the stand of trees southeast of Dry Lake. Climb through them and ski along the gentle slope on the east bank of White Chief Creek. To reach White Chief Bowl, climb along the ravine leading from it and sidehill on its east bank. If you climb up the west side, you will pass some limestone caves with openings to the surface much like crevasses in a glacier. At times the openings are bridged with snow and are dangerous.

From the cirque, head south toward the granite arete. When you have climbed 600′ turn toward the pass. It is a gradual climb on a rounded bench to just below the pass. On the pass you will be able to look southwest down wide, gradual slopes toward Hockett Meadows. The dome to the southwest with the steep east face is Homer's Nose.

Alpine skiers who want to descend by another route can traverse ¾ mile northwest and ski down a steep couloir to Eagle Lake. From Eagle Lake you can either ski directly down to Mineral King Valley or cross a saddle to the west and ski down across the Mosquito Lakes to Mineral King Valley.

South of the Sierra

## TOURING AREA: Southern California

The consistently good skiing south of the Sierra is on or near the tops of mountains. Mount Pinos, San Jacinto and San Gorgonio are mountain oases surrounded by suburbs and the Mojave Desert. Southern snow is variable. The only time one may be sure of skiing powder is during cold storms. The rest of the time you can expect to ski corn or wet new snow. In good snow years there are logging or access roads that provide miles of nordic skiing; icy conditions will make level roads difficult to ski. You wouldn't want to ski off the edge of a road onto a steep hillside. Expect to find ice after a rain or a thaw. A Santa Ana wind will either melt the snow or create a hard, icy snowpack. Some skiers tell of skiing on ice so thick they could see down to the rocks.

Avalanches are uncommon in the southern Transverse Ranges where the warm snow stabilizes rapidly. However, intense tropical storms from the Pacific can create a brief but very high avalanche hazard. Most slides occur during or just after storms when the snow is wet and heavy. Some veteran ski tourers tell of seeing avalanches that began in the high peaks and were flash floods by the time they reached the desert.

A low cloud can cause a whiteout when it envelopes a ridge or mountain top so skiing in fog is common. Carry a map and compass. Rime, which occurs when wet clouds flow over cold trees, snow or rocks is common. When you ski on what appears to be ice cubes it is probably chunks of rime. Most ski touring trailheads are crowded. Parking is limited and rules are strictly enforced. There aren't many ski tourers but there are hordes of snow players all armed with inner-tubes. When you go skiing avoid crowds by arriving very early and leaving early in the afternoon. Skiing in the late afternoon is not very good—the snow ices and crusts up when shadows appear.

Every year the skiing is different. Snow depths and conditions will vary; you may not always find good snow but you will definitely find challenging snow. Experienced southern California ski tourers tend to ski well in difficult conditions. It is fitting that the southern ski touring season begins each year with the Epoke Sand Classic race.

In addition to the tours listed there are more areas to explore. Mountain 'N Air Sports is a new ski touring center in Wrightwood. To find the touring center inquire locally or phone (213) 248-0449. The center will offer rentals, lessons, trail maps plus provide maintained ski trails in the Table Mountain Area to

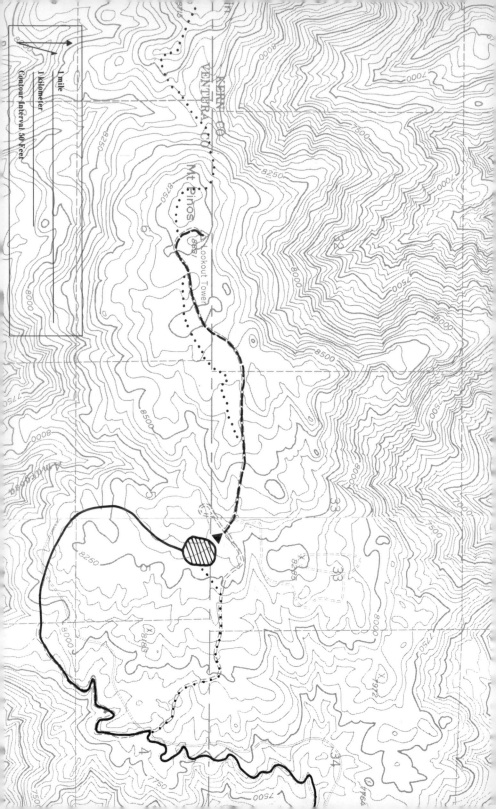

the north of Big Pines. Big Pines is bisected by the San Andreas Fault. The tour out of the Blue Ridge Road is popular; from the road you can see the Panamint Mountains to the east and Santa Catalina Island to the west. Old timers say that you can see the ocean on a clear day. To ski along Blue Ridge, park at Inspiration Point about a mile west of Big Pines on the Angeles Crest Highway. The Pacific Crest Trail also follows Blue Ridge. Be careful when you cross the downhill ski runs. You may have to walk along parts of the road that face south or are too steep to ski.

Buffalo Bills, home of the Big Bear Lake Ski Touring Company, is located west of the Snow Summit turn-off on Highway 18. Ski touring near Big Bear Lake is best on Highway 38 toward Onyx summit. Snow permitting you can ski in the Greenspot campground. Onyx Summit has some nordic terrain but the most popular touring area is Heart Bar, 6 miles down Highway 38 from Onyx Summit. Five miles further on Highway 38 is Jinks Loop Road. In between is Barton Flats. Storms lifted or squeezed around San Gorgonio mountain drop a little extra precipitation on the flats. Most nordic skiers prefer to ski the eastern portion of the flats. More advanced nordic skiers should ski up the Poopout Hill road and even up the San Gorgonio trail to Dry Lake.

Snow Summit now provides a complete cross-country ski center, including rentals, a track system and both flat skiing and nordic downhill lessons.

Nordic downhill lessons are also available at Kratka Ridge.

At Mt. Pinos lessons and rentals are available at Frazier Ski and Pack, located on the right just after the turnoff from I-5.

# TOUR 30

To Mount Pinos (8800′ 2682 m)
From the Mount Pinos parking lot (8200′ 2499 m)
Mileage: 3 miles 5 km
Elevation Gain: 600′ 183 m
Classification: Beginning nordic
Season: Mid December through March
Topo Maps: *7.5 minute series, Sawmill Mountains, Cuddy Valley*

## Features

Mount Pinos at 8831' is the highest peak in Los Padres National Forest. It is usually only visible from the Central Valley. The ski tour follows the Pinos Ridge until it breaks out into several shallow, open alpine bowls ringed with fir, Jeffrey and Limber pines. Considering its elevation and exposure, Mt. Pinos is not very windy. As in other parts of the Transverse Ranges, storms or fog may flow in rapidly. In bad weather the Air Force microwave tower on the summit makes sounds like the wings of wild ducks. Carry a map and compass; it's a long way out if you can't find the parking lot.

Wildlife is abundant in the Los Padres and it's common to see coyote tracks in the snow. In low snow times the tracks of deer and cougar are visible. The Sespe Condor sanctuary is located to the south. Condors may be seen far in the distance soaring over lower hillsides or flying over nearby passes on their way to the Central Valley.

In addition to the beginning tour described there is a more advanced tour to Sawmill Mountain, ½ mile across the saddle between Sawmill and Pinos. Cerro Noroeste, or Mount Abel is 3½ miles to the northwest. According to some skiers the snow on Abel is better than that on Pinos. However, the road to the summit hasn't been plowed for years; the small ski resort has also been closed for some time.

The parking at Mount Pinos is very limited. If you can, carpool and arrive early. Snowcampers should check at the Chuchupate Ranger Station just a few miles up the Stauffer Road. Turn left at the Cuddy Valley turn-off. The road will often be closed so check before you are turned back at Frazier Park. The Forest Service has a twenty-four hour telephone service (805-245-3449) describing snow and road conditions.

## Description

On I-5 take the Frazier Park turn-off to the west. It is about 2 miles north of Gorman. Go 7 miles west on the county road and turn at the Mt. Pinos turn-off. The parking lot is 14 miles up the road. The 50' contours on the 7½ minute maps are misleading for skiers used to 80' contours on 15 minute maps. The terrain is not nearly as steep as you might think.

From the parking lot you may ski to the east along a short snow-covered road that will come out on the plowed road. Once you get beyond the postholing snow players there are several nice areas to set up lesson track loops. The snow-covered road to the summit of Pinos is at the west side of the parking lot. It is less than a mile to the summit meadows along the road which may be icy and crowded. Follow the road to the second meadow where you will be able to see the microwave tower. Past the microwave tower you will come to the windswept condor lookout. There are many fine small areas to ski between the parking lot and the viewpoint. Although small, the area lends itself to exploring. There is a trail back to the parking lot which contours along the hillside below the road. Don't drop too low if you don't know where you are. It would be very easy to ski down the wrong ridge or gully.

# TOUR 31

To San Gorgonio Mountain (11,502′ 3505 m)
From Poopout Hill (7800′ 2377m)
**Mileage:** 14 miles 23 km, round trip
**Elevation Gain:** 3700′ 1128 m
**Classification:** Intermediate-to-difficult alpine
**Season:** Mid-April to late May
**Topo Map:** *San Gorgonio Mountain*
**Wilderness Permit:** Obtain from Forest Service in San
   Bernardino or at Mill Creek, Camp Angelus or Barton Flats

# Features

San Gorgonio Mountain, or Old Greyback, as it is locally  known, is one of the most popular alpine tours in Southern California. The tour is in the San Gorgonio Wilderness, a high wilderness oasis in the technological Southland. The area's wilderness status prevented the building of a ski resort during the early Sixties. The Forest Service and conservation organizations, which are often at odds, both opposed the ski resort proposal.

A warm Santa Ana wind can rapidly thaw a cold snowpack and cause damp avalanches. In addition, the wind can rapidly melt or evaporate the snowpack. At times wind has removed the entire snowpack here, bringing an early end to the skiing season.

The avalanche hazard can be very high on this tour. There are even small slide paths crossing the route into Dry Lake. Wait for a week after a storm to give the snow time to form an unbreakable sun crust (corn snow).

# Description

Leave the San Bernardino Freeway (Interstate 10) at Redlands, and take Highway 38 through Camp Angelus. Nine miles past Camp Angelus, turn right on the Jenks Lake road and follow the road to the parking lot at Poopout Hill. The road is usually free of snow by mid-March.

It is not uncommon to have to carry skis for the first mile or so up the South Fork Meadows trail. From the south side of the parking lot, climb over a small hill. Heading southeast, gradually climb beside the South Fork. After a mile, the route comes close to the creek and then climbs to South Fork Meadows.

Above the meadows, the ponderosa pine and white fir begin to give way to lodgepole pine. Cross to the southeast edge of the meadows and climb southeast. After ¼ mile turn more to the east and follow the south side of the draw up to Dry Lake, which makes a good base camp.

See whether you can distinguish between ponderosa and Jeffrey pine. The easiest way is by inspecting the cones. Jeffrey cones are larger, and the prickles at the ends of their scales point inward. Ponderosa cones are smaller, and their prickles face outward. Hold the cone in your hand; if it pricks you, it's ponderosa.

From a base camp at Dry Lake, it is possible in favorable conditions to climb the north face of San Gorgonio Mountain directly to the summit. If the snow is hard, you will need an ice axe and crampons. To climb the classic route up San Gorgonio, ascend the gully at the south end of the lake. From the top of the gully, traverse west below the north face until you come to the base of the Big Draw. Climb the Big Draw to the main ridge. It is very steep just below the ridge. Ski east along the ridge to the summit. The skiing down during the afternoon should be good.

In early spring or in a cold period when other slopes are icy, the ascent of Charlton Peak provides a safe alternative climb. Traverse past the Big Draw, to the west, staying below the runouts from avalanche paths until you come to the foot of a gully between Jepson and Charlton peaks. Climb the moderately steep gully through open timber to the ridge at the head of it. The summit of Charlton Peak is a short distance northwest. On clear days this tour is in sunlight from early morning until midafternoon. If you leave your pack at the bottom of the gully instead of at Dry Lake, you can ski down a marked trail directly to South Fork Meadows.

# TOUR 32

To San Jacinto Peak (10,804′ 3293 m)
From the Top of the Palm Springs Tramway (8500′ 2591 m)
Mileage: 7 miles 11 km, round trip
Elevation Gain: 2300′ 701 m
Classification: Intermediate nordic; the final mile
  to the summit is intermediate alpine
Season: Early March to late April
Topo Map: *Palm Springs*

## Features

The key to this tour is timing it so there is snow. Even after a storm the snow is not always reliable. The inland location and the warm Santa Ana winds keep the snow shallow.

The view is different from what one associates with skiing; in addition to the San Bernardino Mountains, on a clear day you can see the warm colors of the surrounding desert. Nordic skiers can find many places to explore.

This is one of the few tours on which you have to ride a tram. You can hike the 5900' that the tram rises, but that trip is never a ski tour. The tram does not run every day; call ahead.

## Description

From the San Bernardino Freeway (Interstate 10) take Highway 111 toward Palm Springs. At the north edge of town, turn west on the Palm Springs Aerial Tram road. If you plan to stay overnight, ask the parking lot attendant where to park. From the Mountain Station, the upper tram terminus, go to the ranger station for a permit.

From the ranger station ski west through the forest. Sugar pine and white fir are common along the creek. After ¾ mile, head in a more southwesterly direction for another ¾ mile, to Round Valley, where camping is permitted.

An alternative route is to ski south from the Mountain Station for ¾ mile and then turn west. You will come to Round Valley after ¾ mile more.

Skiers who don't want to camp at Round Valley should keep on a more westward course from the Mountain Station, directly toward Tamarack Valley. As this name suggests, lodgepole (formerly called tamarack) pine is common here.

From the valley climb the southeast slope toward the saddle between Mt. San Jacinto and Miller Peak. From the saddle follow the ridge west until you reach the summit of San Jacinto. For a pleasant side trip, ski from the saddle over to Jean Peak and back.

The Palm Spring Ski Touring Center (619) 481-7547 is located near the top terminal of the tram. The center provides rentals, lessons and maintains ski trails in Long Valley. Trail information and snow conditions plus maps are available at the center. The tram is open seven days a week and a ticket costs $8.95.

Trans-Sierra Tours

## Trans-Sierra Tours

There is an aspect of California ski touring many skiers never experience. The Sierra high country in winter is remote and difficult to visit. It is interesting to note that California, a populous and technologically advanced state, has a vast inaccessible winter wilderness. You have to go to the far north to find comparable ski touring terrain.

The High Sierra is unbroken by plowed roads from Carson Pass to Walker Pass near Tehachapi. It is one continuous mountain massif; a winter wall between California and the deserts to the east. For much of its length, the lowest passes are at least 9,000′ high. Between the high crest and the deep U-shaped valleys there are plateau uplands which are rarely skied. Most Californians accustomed to skiing the meadows and forests don't realize there is so much good skiing further into the backcountry. You have to go on more than a two-day tour to reach most of the good high country. Loop tours into this country are the most practical but trans-Sierra tours hold a particular attraction. There is a special romance about a trans-Sierra ski tour. Where else can you leave the high desert, climb above timberline, ski over ridges and along glaciated canyons, descend to the Sequoia trees on the west slope and end up in orange groves and vineyards. Many of the sections of this book — Snowcamping, Survival Skiing, the equipment lists are derived from practical experience gained on High Sierra tours.

When you plan a trans-Sierra tour think of it as an expedition. Logistics are important. Adequate food (4,000 calories per day per person) and emergency gear and plans are essential. I have seen a supposedly indestructible ski break in half 45 miles and two passes from the nearest assistance. We remounted the binding and I skied on one seven foot ski and one four foot ski.

Most trans-Sierra tours are not too difficult or dangerous for a physically fit and experienced party. Many tour parties have traveled the High Sierra. Orland Bartholomew's epic tour of the Sierra Crest took place in 1928-29. He carried a heavy pack even though he had 11 caches. Part of his pack was a twelve-pound down robe. The popular touring routes were first skied in the late 20's and early 30's. Otto Steiner skied from Giant Forest to Mount Whitney in five days; a tour which was repeated in 1966 by a group of National Park Rangers. In the early 30's, Milana Jank and Dennis Jones skied from Lee Vining to Yosemite in two days. In 1975 two Norwegians skiing in tracks left by an earlier skiing party, went from Mammoth Mountain to Yosemite Valley in one long day. The Tahoe-Yosemite Trail was skied in the early 30's. No one knows for sure where Snowshoe Thompson or some of his friends might have skied; one has the feeling that an adventurous gold miner could have skied the entire Sierra Crest in 1850 and never bothered to tell anyone about it.

There are other tours in addition to the ones described. Snow Survey parties have skied over Cottonwood and Siberia Passes for years. They ski up to Tyndall Creek and then back. The High Route described could be skied by way of Mount Whitney. The tour up over Shepherd Pass across the Bighorn Plateau down into the Kern Canyon and up Rattlesnake Creek over Franklin Pass into Mineral King is long and interesting. Susan Beck and Kathy Crandall skied it in the spring of 1979. In the Kings Canyon there is good skiing in the Muir Pass area.

In addition to the equipment listed you may need mountaineering gear. On the Sierra High Route you will definitely need rope, ice axes, crampons and a few carabiners and slings. Even on the easiest backcountry tour it is wise to have an ice axe and 100′ of 7 or 8 mm climbing rope.

There are many pleasures on a long tour. After a few days your sense of values and reality change. Alarm clocks and rush hour traffic become unreal. Your immediate environment is what matters. You get to know your companions in a way you never would in the city. Dinner becomes very important — it's a constant topic. You develop a sense of independence and adventure. Somehow you're a little bit more alive when you reach the top of a pass, see distant peaks and anticipate a good run down to a campsite.

# TOUR 33

To Huntington Lake (7200′ 2195 m)
From North Lake (9380′ 2859 m)
Mileage: 45 miles 72 km, shuttle tour
Elevation Gain: Large and variable
Classification: Difficult nordic
Season: Mid-March to early April
Topo Maps: *Mt. Goddard, Mt. Tom, Mt. Abbott,
    Blackcap Mountain, Kaiser Peak*
Wilderness Permit: Obtain in Bishop

## Features

Except for lower Piute Canyon, this tour is ideal for nordic skiers. They will be able to stretch their legs on the long, gentle slopes. Tourers on alpine skis will find little steep downhill terrain and many long, easy slopes.

This tour should be made early enough so there is still adequate snow both along the San Joaquin River and on Florence Lake (7300′). Study the weather reports from the Fresno region. Snow reports from the China Peak ski area will give you some idea of how much snow to expect.

Take at least a week's supply of food, although with clear weather and good snow, the tour should take five leisurely days. Storms and deep snow may increase the time and effort needed, particularly in crossing the avalanche paths in lower Piute Canyon. On ideal snow, expert nordic skiers can probably ski the whole 45 miles in two very long days.

## Description

From North Lake climb west past gullied Mt. Emerson to Piute Pass. (See Tour 14 for a complete description.) From Piute Pass ski down and across Summit Lake, passing a snowcourse. Mt. Humphreys (almost 14,000′), to the north, and the Glacier Divide (13,000′), to the south, give the view an alpine, top-of-the-world feeling. If weather permits, one may camp here and enjoy the view down Piute Canyon with the Pinnacles towering over the deep canyon. However, wood, shelter and possibly water will be found lower down, along Piute Creek.

Ski down to the right of the creek. Don't try to traverse too far around to the right: it won't be worth the effort. The skiing is good along the creek. To the northeast you can see some

avalanche chutes. There is a controversy about the origin of these wide, shallow chutes. They were probably formed by a combination of avalanches, nivation (freeze-thaw) and other processes. Perhaps small hanging glaciers were the main cause.

Continue down the canyon. The snow surface on the south side of the creek may offer better skiing. The run down along Piute Creek offers some of the most pleasant skiing on the whole tour. As you round the bend opposite French Canyon and Hutchinson Meadow, you pass a wide slide path that comes down almost to the south side of the creek. The young trees living along the path have been limbed by avalanches. A medium-sized avalanche must occur every few years in this area. If the paths slid too often, there would be no trees on the hillside, and If the path slid very seldom—say, every 20 years—the trees would be much larger. The most obvious large avalanche paths may be active only for a few minutes every five years or so.

From Hutchinson Meadow ski southwest along the north side of the creek, approximately following the summer trail. Because of the southern exposure you may encounter bare patches here during a low-snow year.

The next 3 miles pass through a steep, narrow, avalanche-prone canyon. If you approach this area late in the day, you will be wise to camp somewhere above it in the timber. Cross the hazardous area in the morning when the snowpack is frozen, unless a storm is approaching. New snow might make lower Piute Canyon too hazardous to descend, forcing you to wait several days or turn back.

Ski down the canyon along the bench that the summer trail follows. Don't go along the creek unless you are confident that the snow will not collapse. Just before you reach Turret Creek, carefully cross Piute Creek and work your way down the east bank to the San Joaquin River, where you can cross the bridge back to the west bank.

Each party will find this deep canyon in a different condition, and the particular conditions might necessitate a slightly different route from the one described here. That is why this tour is rated difficult. You should expect to have to wander around a bit and do a little reconnoitering.

From the confluence of Piute Creek and the San Joaquin River, the rest of the tour is ideal nordic skiing. On the way to Florence Lake you pass through Jeffrey pine and lodgepole, with aspen and fir in the damper locations. Just beyond Blaney Hot Springs you encounter the buildings of the Muir Trail

Ranch. Something always seems to be lost when you see buildings after a tour into a wild area.

From Blaney Meadows follow the trail until Florence Lake comes into view — more precisely, its bed. The lake is drained every fall to catch the spring runoff and maintain a steady flow of water to hydroelectric systems.

Ski down to the lake bed and head northwest toward the outlet, where you will pass more buildings and the particularly conspicuous dam. Climb the hillside between the dam and the cluster of buildings. The road to Huntington Lake begins here.

Once you are sure that you are on the road, it is a long, easy tour to Kaiser Pass, 17 miles away. The last few miles to the pass are moderate uphill climbing. There is one bowl just before the pass which is dangerous during avalanche hazard. For a description from Kaiser Pass down, see Tour 24.

Kaweah Crest

# TOUR: 34

To Yosemite Valley (4000′ 1219 m)
From Mammoth Lakes (8900′ 2713 m)
Mileage: 42 miles 68 km
Elevation Gain: varies, Donohue Pass at 11,056′ highest point
Classification: Strong intermediate nordic
Season: Mid-March through April
Topo Maps: *Devils Postpile, Mono Craters, Tuolumne Meadows, Hetch Hetchy*
Wilderness Permit: Obtain in Mammoth

## Features

This is one of the most popular trans-Sierra routes; it is one of the few routes where you are likely to see other skiers. The route passes through scenic and varied terrain. Banner Peak is very imposing from Thousand Island Lake. The run down from Donohue Pass is usually good — ski it in the morning. The tour through Tuolumne Meadows and down the Tioga Road to Snow Creek is fairly level; with a track and good snow it goes fast. Tenaya Lake in winter is beautiful. There is usually a ranger in the Tuolumne Meadows Ranger Station.

## Description

There are many variations of this route. The quickest way to Tuolumne Meadows is up the Tioga Pass Road. The Mono Pass route is almost as fast but considerably more interesting and less avalanche prone. The classic route begins at the Mammoth Mountain ski resort parking lot and heads down the road to Agnew Meadows. (Overnight parking is not allowed at the ski resort.) Behind the Agnew Meadows pack station climb a short gully to a shelf and follow the shelf system along the high trail to Badger Lakes. From there it is an easy tour up to Thousand Island Lake. Don't get too low; stay above the steep area above Lake Olaine.

You will probably need to study your map. Most winters you will find running water in the streams coming off Two Teats and San Joaquin Mountain. The climb up to Island Pass from Thousand Island Lake is easy. From Island Pass traverse to the northwest across a ridge before you ski down to Rush Creek. The side tour down Rush Creek to June Lake is steep but direct. Don't try it if an avalanche hazard exists. The southern half of Gem Lake is surrounded by cliffs; ski to the north shore.

5 miles

5 kilometers

Contour Interval 200 Feet

The climb to Donohue Pass is in the open during the last few
hundred feet. On the ski down there is one steep bowl just
before Tuolumne Meadows; it could be icy or avalanche prone.
Don't underestimate the time needed to ski the length of the
meadows; it could be slow going in difficult snow. A lay-over
day in the meadows is well worth your time. On the road you
will probably see other ski tracks and if you're unfortunate you
will have to ski down the tracks of the snow ranger's snowcat.
As you ski down Snow Creek you will run out of snow near the
rim of Yosemite Valley. Follow the Snow Creek trail down into
Yosemite Valley.

# TOUR 35

The Sierra High Route
To Giant Forest (7200' 2194 m)
From Symmes Creek (6400' 1950 m)
Mileage: 35 miles 56 km
Elevation Gain: large
Classification: Expert nordic, strong intermediate alpine
Season April-May
Topo Maps: *Mount Whitney, Triple Divide Peak*
Wilderness Permit: Obtain at Lone Pine Ranger Station

## Features

This tour begins in the high desert and ends in the Sequoia groves of Giant Forest. The route winds along the Western Divide staying above timberline for three days. You cross nine passes or ridges, the highest, near Milestone Peak, is 13,000'. This is a classic tour because it stays high; the lowest point on the tour is the drop down to the headwaters of the Kern at 10,500'. If there was to be a Haute Route in the United States, this would be it.

The route is close to the one followed by Otto Steiner in 1931. Steiner and other parties who followed him traveled from the west and dropped down to the Kern-Kaweah from Triple Divide Peak to Junction Meadow. From Junction Meadow they climbed Wallace Creek to the Muir trail where they skied on to Whitney or Shepherd Pass. The High Route described here was first discovered by Nick Hartzell who hiked it in the 60's and together with David Beck and Bob Couly, skied it for the first time in 1975. The route has been skied with both alpine and nordic skis. Expect ice, slush, breakable crust and excellent corn snow.

## Description

To reach Symmes Creek trailhead drive north from Independence on the Kearsarge Pass Road. After four miles turn left onto the Symmes Creek road. After a mile and a half take the right hand fork. In another mile you will pass the horse corrals. Within another half mile take the right hand fork leading up to the trailhead parking lot. You can also reach the trailhead by a series of roads from Camp Manzanar, a Japanese detention camp dating from World War II. All that is left of the camp are some old untended fruit trees, the entrance gate, and a sobering monument.

You will have to walk the first few miles up the impressive Symmes Creek gorge. A proper way to start the tour. After hiking a mile turn to the south and climb up the steep hillside to the ridge above Shepherd Creek. The snow conditions on the shady hillside are often poor. From the ridge follow the trail to Mahogany Flat and Anvil Camp. If you lose the trail, plan on spending a few extra hours bushwhacking. From Anvil Camp work your way up to Shepherd Pass. The sunny slopes are generally safer and easier going. To cross the pass climb up to the left of the rock cliff in the middle of the pass. Cross over to the rock and pass through a notch in the base of the rock and walk up on a wind-blown hollow along the cliff's side. Then walk up the short, steep snow slope on the left to the top of Shepherd Pass. The run down to Tyndall Creek is easy. Drop around the base of Diamond Mesa; stay above the two groves of Foxtail pine. Then ski in an easterly direction to the rim of the Kern Canyon. Follow the summer trail course; keep to the northeast. The upper Kern is very scenic. There is wood and water along the Kern River. Ski down the river to an elevation of 10,500′ then ski up alongside Milestone Creek. The next pass, at 13,000′ is to the left or southeast of the peak. The wide saddle is best approached from the right. You may need an ice axe and rope to get over it.

Milestone Bowl, on the other side of the pass, is a good ski run. Ski down the bowl to the 11,200′ contour and then climb a saddle three-fourths of a mile south or to the left, of Colby Pass. The pass, at 12,000′ is not quite as steep as it looks. Once over it, contour around and ski down to a small lake. Then ski down to about the 11,300′ level to avoid some rock bands. Climb up to the obvious pass at 12,200′. To the left, or south is Triple Divide Peak. From the pass there is a short steep run down to Glacier Lake.

You are now skiing in the Kings River drainage. The large cliff to the west of Glacier Lake can be difficult to get around. You may either traverse a steep area half way down it or ski all the way to the gully at its base. Climb back up and traverse across the upper cirque of Cloud Canyon and ski towards the point where the cornice ends on Glacier Ridge. This ridge is different every year, sometimes it is an easy climb and other years it is steep. Once on the ridge walk to the north over a small hump until you can see all the way down to the Deadman Canyon. Ski toward the pass at 11,300′ to the north of horn peak, 11,830′. Cross over the pass and ski down to the north of the unnamed lake.

You are now in the headwaters of the middle fork of the Kaweah. Ski to the southwest until you are at the base of the cliff below peak 11,598'. The view to the south is of the severely glaciated Western Divide. Farewell Gap is the prominent V-shaped notch. Ski west and climb about two hundred feet and cross an easy pass above Buck Canyon. To the west you can see the Santa Lucias in the Coast Range. Now traverse to the northwest across the Tableland. Ski down across Table Meadows and on down the Marble Fork of the Kaweah.

You will be skiing in timber for the first time in several days. You will feel the effect of thicker air and relief from the intense sunlight. At the 9,600' elevation, climb the small hump to the left of the river to a low pass and ski directly down to Pear Lake Hut. Information about the route to Giant Forest and hut reservations may be found in the Pear Lake Tour description.

Triple Divide Peak

# Index

# Bibliography

David Brower, ed. *The Sierra Club Manual of Ski Mountaineering.* Ballantine Books, New York 1969.

Caldwell, John, *Cross Country Skiing Today.* The Stephen Greene Press, 1977.

Kjellstrom, Bjorn, *Be Expert With Map and Compass.*

Manning, Harvey ed., *Mountaineering: The Freedom of the Hills.* The Mountaineers, Seattle, 1967.

Monteverdi, *Synoptic Meteorology of California Weather Anomalies.* Cal Books.

Murie, Olaus, *Field Guide to Animal Tracks.*

Rees, David, *Cross Country Skiing.* Chilton Book Company 1975.

Roper, Steve, *The Climbers Guide to the High Sierra,* Sierra Club Books 1976.

Schumacher Smith, Genny, *Deepest Valley.* William Kaufmann, Inc., 1978.

Storer, Tracy and Unsinger, Robert, *Sierra Nevada Natural History.* U.C. Press.

Tejada-Flores, Lito and Allen Steck, *Wilderness Skiing.* Sierra Club, 1972.

United States Forest Service, *Avalanche Handbook*

Whitney, Stephen, *A Sierra Club Naturalists Guide: The Sierra Nevada.* Sierra Club, 1979.

Wilderness Press publishes summer hiking guides to every part of the state.
University of California Press has a comprehensive list of Natural History Guides.

The End